EXPLOSIVE
GOLF

Using the Science of Kinesiology to Improve Your Swing

Library of Congress Cataloging-in-Publication Data

Yessis, Michael.
     Explosive golf : using the science of kinesiology to improve
your swing / Michael Yessis.
          p.   cm.
     ISBN 1-57028-223-4
     1. Swing (Golf)   2. Golf—Training.   3. Golf—Physiological
aspects.   I. Title.
     GV979.S9 Y47 1998
     796.352'3—dc21

                                        98-29484
                                           CIP

Please note that the quality of the images reproduced in this book is because a digital video camera was used to capture the action of the golf swing. The author and publisher believe that this method of capturing the images is best suited to the purpose and intention of the book. The digital camera captures motion better than any other photographic medium easily available today, though the images do not reproduce as well as conventional images.

Cover design by Todd Petersen
Interior design by Precision Graphics
Interior photographs by Michael Yessis

Published by Masters Press
A division of NTC/Contemporary Publishing Group, Inc.
4255 West Touhy Avenue, Lincolnwood (Chicago), Illinois 60712-1975 U.S.A.
Printed in the United States of America
International Standard Book Number: 1-57028-223-4

  00   01   02   03   04   05   VL 20 19 18 17 16 15 14 13 12 11 10   9   8   7   6   5   4   3   2

Contents

Preface

Anyone can play golf. The first time you went out to play, you probably shot about 150, but it was fun. But now that you are a serious student of golf, you want to improve your game so that you can consistently break 100 or, better yet, shoot in the 80s or below. To do this, you need to develop a good swing and duplicate the same basic swing on every shot.

Doing this is not as easy as it may seem. If you listen to conventional wisdom, you will get better clubs, take more lessons, and have more practice. Many golfers have tried these routes, and some have spent hours on the golf range trying to get their bodies into the positions recommended by the pros. Eventually, they ended up even more frustrated! As you have probably experienced, making changes, especially when you have a set swing, is often very hard and can be very costly.

There is, however, a very simple way of improving the golf swing. Regardless of the clubs you use or the recommendations given to you by a golf pro, you must have the physical ability to hit the ball as far and as accurately as you desire. You must have the strength, flexibility, and coordination to do this. If you do not, you are doomed to failure regardless of how much money you spend, lessons you take, and practice you put in. Your swing is only as good as your physical abilities will allow.

Making a few simple changes to improve your abilities will improve your game beyond your wildest expectations. This book will show you how you can do this. You will also gain the ability to carry out the recommendations given to you not only by the pros, but in this book.

As director of strength and conditioning at the Professional Golfers Career College in Temecula, California, I have seen many golfers significantly improve their distance, accuracy, and consistency by improving their physical abilities. Most noticeable were improvements in strength, speed of movement, flexibility, and coordination. As a result, it was not uncommon to see the average shot distance increase by 30 to 60 yards. Some golfers improved to such an extent that they could easily hit 300 yards into the wind!

By doing special exercises, golfers who had typically experienced back pain during or after playing found that their pain soon disappeared. Still others found it much easier to maintain their stance and balance during the swing because of a stronger support base and greater control of and feel for their muscle actions. In fact, without exception, every single golfer saw improvement in his or her game after undertaking a specialized strength and flexibility program specific to his or her swing actions.

Many players got into a routine of doing daily morning exercises (taking no more than five to ten minutes), while others made time in their hectic schedules to work out two to three times per week for a weekly total of no more than 90 to 120 minutes. This is all the time that is needed to show significant improvement in your physical capabilities, which can result in better and more powerful swings.

Reading this book may be the first step on your pathway to playing a great game and getting the fullest possible amount of enjoyment and satisfaction from the game. Going over the key exercises and explanations in the book can be the difference between trying to swing better and actually doing it.

By incorporating the concepts presented in this book, you will be amazed at how much progress you can make in a relatively short time. This applies not only to simply making changes in the golf swing, but also to fixing any particular physical problems that you may have. For example, many golfers are plagued by lower back problems. But lower back problems are some of the easiest to take care of! Although this may sound hard to believe, it has been proven time and time again—not only with golfers, but with athletes in other sports as well. In this book, you will see how this is done so that you, too, can play pain-free and have the greatest swing possible.

Although this book contains a great deal of high-level information, I have made a serious attempt to present it in a very simple and straightforward manner. It is well illustrated, not only with photos of the golf swing, but also with pictures of the exercises that are specific to the key actions in the swing. Thus you should not think of this book as only a book on special exercises for golf; rather, you should approach it as something that will give you a much better understanding of the golf swing and how you can improve it easily and in the shortest amount of time.

The ball is on the tee. Do you wish to attack it and hit it farther than ever before, or would you rather continue to swing the same old way and achieve the same old results? Your success or failure is up to you! If you get involved in this book, I can guarantee you will see amazing results.

Acknowledgments

I am deeply indebted to many people. Without their assistance this book would have been impossible to complete. The order in which the names appear is not related to the importance of the work and assistance they provided. More specifically, I would like to thank

- Dr. Kenny Baird, who introduced me to the Professional Golfers Career College and who served as one of the professional golfers whose swing photos appear in this book.
- Dr. Tim Somerville, president and founder of the Professional Golfers Career College, who gave me the opportunity to use my program with his students, assisted in its development, and for his input on the book.
- Kent Brown, executive director of the Professional Golfers Career College and professional golfer, whose swing pictures appear in this book and who found students at the college to serve as models, which was a great help. Also for his suggestions regarding the book.
- Wayne Searle, master instructor at Kip Puterbaugh's Aviara Golf Academy, who executed many swings for use in this book.
- Johji Furuki, Japanese professional tour player, whose swing pictures appear in this book.

- Dave Ducommon, exercise model and graduate of the Professional Golfers Career College, who now plays on the Asian tour.
- Cristy Keinick, exercise model and graduate, Professional Golfers Career College.
- Mark Hoesing, exercise model and graduate, Professional Golfers Career College.
- Jerry Singleton, exercise model and a great golfer who looks as good in his pictures as he does on the course.
- Marissa Yessis, golfer and exercise model, who served as my computer operator and worked diligently importing the pictures from the camera into the computer and preparing them for publication.
- Tim Eberlein, PGA, director of golf at the San Diego Golf Academy, who helped in getting additional models on short notice.
- Tom McGimpsey, exercise model and graduate, San Diego Golf Academy. He is now a professional in Connecticut.
- Mike Shaffer, exercise model and graduate, San Diego Golf Academy. He is now a professional in Texas.
- Masaki Yonetani for introducing me to Johji and other Japanese tour players and the Impact Builder.

- Terry Singleton for legal advice and his insightful comments on the book.
- John Boehme, computer specialist, without whose assistance in selecting the programs and working out the bugs I would not have known what to do.
- Edie Yessis, my dear wife who persevered through many readings, checking on content and construction. Without her continued support, my work would not have been as interesting.
- Astar Inc., Golf Training Systems for their help in getting good pictures from analysis tapes.
- Julia Anderson, project editor, NTC/Contemporary Publishing, who worked closely with me in finalizing the book.
- Ken Samelson, acquisitions editor, NTC/Contemporary Publishing, who was helpful in easing the transition from Masters Press to NTC/Contemporary.
- Tom Bast, former publisher of Masters Press who wanted to have this book published.

Your Swing Potential

Defining the Challenge

There are probably more how-to books and articles written on golf than on any other sport. This attests not only to the popularity of golf, but also to its individuality. There are almost as many different golf swings as there are different golf courses. It is precisely this element of individuality as it relates to the golf swing, however, that often leads to confusion among players.

There is much disagreement in regard to defining the key actions executed in the golf swing, not to mention the timing and sequence in which those actions occur. As a result, many common questions arise: What constitutes an effective swing? What is the most effective means to enhance performance? How can a player best avoid injury?

I once had a golfer tell me he had been to fifty different teaching pros in search of a better understanding of the golf swing. Each pro told him something different about his swing, compounding the confusion. One explanation for this scenario is simple—often a pro considers his swing (or that which he teaches) to be the ideal model of execu-

tion. The fact is, there's no such thing as the "perfect" swing.

Regardless of the particular type of swing or the player, however, there are specific key actions that everyone must execute in order to attain a successful result. Your physical capabilities determine how much you rely on each of these actions. These capabilities also determine your range of motion and influence the sequence and timing of the actions that are emphasized in your swing. This became quite evident as I analyzed the swings of hundreds of professional golfers. Ultimately, physical factors affect your potential for improvement, level of fitness, and vulnerability to injury.

Because each golfer appeared to emphasize certain key actions, it was difficult to identify an "ideal" swing. Almost all the golfers appeared to rely on a few key elements and often had some negative aspects present in their swing. For example, one golfer had a great backswing and initial downswing and showed distinct separation between body action and the buildup of force in the swing. However, the same golfer would straighten his left leg and raise his body just before impact. Other golfers, on the other hand, showed little separation between hip rotation and shoulder rotation during the swing. The list of distinct and subtle differences in the swing is as long as the list of individual golfers.

What this proved to me is that every golfer is capable of improving his or her swing regardless of how talented the player is. I have yet to meet someone who could not become a better player. The key is to determine what your strong and weak points are and then take the necessary steps to address them. This includes changes not only in technique, but also in physical abilities.

Analysis Versus Description

The most accurate way to determine the key actions involved in the swing is to analyze biomechanically and kinesiologically some of the best hitters playing the game and then evaluate which actions and sequences these players use. Although it is not uncommon to read a description of what occurs in the swing, an analysis is something altogether different. An analysis answers questions such as: If the swing is effective, why is it effective? What is the role of each joint action? Which actions can be changed to make the technique more effective? How can the specific actions be made more powerful? Should the swing be modified at all? If so, how? Most sources of standard instruction fail to address important points such as these.

Rarely is there agreement among the pros as to why a particular action is necessary in the swing. Why must a specific action occur or precede another action? Why is a certain action more effective than another? In what way is it best executed? Seldom is there agreement when identifying the best sequence of actions needed to produce maximum force. Seldom is there conformity when determining how each action contributes to the production of maximum force. Instead, we see articles espousing the opinions of golf pros who are often at odds with one another's views. In many cases, the information presented is not even based on scientific facts.

I am confident that you have come into contact with articles dealing with certain obvious issues—for

instance, whether the legs, hips, or arms initiate the swing. From biomechanics and kinesiology, we can determine a definitive answer. *Biomechanics* is the study of movement or, more specifically, the movement involved in sport technique. It deals mainly with physical factors such as speed, mass, acceleration, levers, force, and so on, including the physiological functions during the movement. Some think of biomechanics as the science of movement based on principles from physics and anatomy. It explains the why of movement and how movements can be improved through scientifically-based modifications. *Kinesiology* is the study of human motion and deals mainly with the muscles and muscle functions. It describes movement, which muscles are involved in the movement, and how they are involved. It explores muscular involvement in sport technique, while biomechanics looks at the physical factors involved in the movement.

In attempting to pinpoint the source of the effective swing, we know that only one of these anatomical sources can initiate it—it is the hip action in the hip slide (weight shift). The leg action is a consequence of the hips moving forward and turning; any arm action must follow if it is to contribute force to the swing.

By applying basic scientific laws, it is possible to come up with accurate descriptions not only of what should take place in the swing, but also of the role that each key action should play. The aforementioned example is just one of the key features that I have included in this book, one basic principle that applies to all swings.

The Golf Swing

For this book, I analyzed the swings of many professionals. In an attempt to be as objective as possible, the key swing actions and the specific instances in which they occur were identified through high-speed videotaping and consequent frame-by-frame analysis of the tapes.

In addition to these means, I used the ASTAR Swing Analysis System to illustrate various graphic details. Superimposed vectors were used to show the displacement of various body parts, the degree of rotation, and the swing plane used by the golfers. Because of the simultaneous taping of individual golfers from two views (front and side) and the comparison of different golfers at the same moment in the swing, it was possible to determine not only the main actions involved in the swing, but also the range of motion and speed of movement.

Photo illustrations were selected to identify the key actions, and special strength and flexibility exercises were created to duplicate these actions. The range of motion, type of muscular contraction, and sequence of the action were all taken into consideration.

In general, golfers differ somewhat in their execution of key movements and the actions they accentuate in each individual swing. Professional golf instructor Dr. Jim Suttie, who completed an extensive study of professional golfers, identified seven different swing types. The results of his characterizations are summarized in the following models:

1. **The arc model.** This player is characterized by a wide arc and upright plane. The swing usually involves a great deal of shoulder and hip rotation on the backswing. Golfers who exemplify this style: Jack Nicklaus and Betsy King.

2. **The muscular advantage model.** This player relies on a strong upper body to hit the ball and is usually referred to as a hitter or a right-sided, down-the-line player. Golfers who exemplify this style: Arnold Palmer and Craig Stadler. (To some extent, Tiger Woods fits into this category.)

3. **The mechanical advantage model.** This player uses leverage (wrist cocking) and body rotation to create power. Golfers who exemplify this style: Nick Faldo and Nick Price. (To some extent, Tiger Woods fits into this category.)

4. **The open-faced model.** This player has a very open face throughout the entire backswing and tries to release the hands and arms early from the top of the swing in order to square up the clubface. A golfer who exemplifies this style: Cory Pavin.

5. **The shut-faced model.** This player has a very closed clubface throughout the entire swing and always has a big turn with the body on the backswing. The swing plane is usually very flat. Such a player has a blocked hand and arm release throughout impact. Golfers who exemplify this style: Paul Azinger and Lee Trevino.

6. **The lateral slider model.** This player has a great deal of slide motion that precedes body rotation. A very wide stance that allows the player to turn over the back leg is typical. Golfers who exemplify this style: Curtis Strange and Peter Jacobson. (Tiger Woods also uses this technique.)

7. **The pure rotational model.** This player seems to rotate the body around a single axis in the upper spine. The arms stay in close to the body on both the backswing and downswing, and a great deal of clubhead velocity is generated in a very circular swing. Golfers who exemplify this style: Mac O'Grady, Jody Mudd, and Chip Beck.

Improving Your Swing

When you want to improve your swing, your inclination is probably to seek out the services of a good teaching pro. If he has a trained eye and knows what to look for, he will be able to spot problem areas and point out necessary changes. If you are then able to carry these recommendations out, you may find that they make a noticeable difference in your swing.

Better equipment, especially clubs designed to fit your individual abilities, can also improve the quality of hits. Extra clubhead weight, larger clubheads, and better balance characteristics can certainly increase hitting distance. Even mental techniques such as shot visualization and relaxation can improve your swing. All these aids are useless, however, unless you can successfully perform the physical movements required to hit a golf ball.

Making progress in terms of your physical abilities plays the most important role in developing a good swing and helping you play up to your potential. For example, improving your ability to execute simple actions such as weight shift and hip rotation will show a positive change in your total swing technique. Improvement in your physical abilities specific to your golf swing is a relatively simple and extremely effective method of bettering your game that has not yet been fully explored.

When you improve upon those physical capabilities specific to the golf swing, you will see a dramatic change in your swing. You will then be able to derive greater benefit from your equipment. Confidence in your ability to execute the necessary shots will in turn grow as you develop a stronger and more powerful swing.

Most golfers have not yet been introduced to the world of beneficial changes that are possible from golf-specific enhancement of their physical capabilities. Instead of improving upon physical qualities, most golf pros tend to recommend dramatic technique changes in order to make up for inferior hitting distance that results from a lack of strength and flexibility. One of the most common examples of this type of problem is hip rotation. Many golfers, especially seniors, suffer from diminished ability to rotate the hips and shoulders fully.

Rather than do simple exercises to regain midsection flexibility and strength, many pros advocate an exaggerated weight shift to produce more force. Not only does an exaggerated weight shift lead to countless other problems, it fails to address the physical losses that these golfers naturally experience.

Keep this in mind: dramatic changes in technique are extremely difficult to accomplish at any age, especially in the senior years. Fortunately, there is a much simpler and more effective solution to the problem. This book will demonstrate that executing a few simple exercises can quickly bring back the flexibility and strength necessary to maintain a consistent swing.

Whenever I think of individual physical abilities, I recall the stories I heard many years ago of "3 Iron Louie." Louie played golf with only one club—the 3 iron. He would make outrageous bets against players who had fourteen or fifteen clubs in their bags, and would usually beat them. Here was a classic example illustrating that it is not a player's clubs that produce the best scores, but the player's ability to handle the clubs.

The more you can improve your physical abilities to develop a better swing, the more effective your game can be. Regardless of the club you use, you must still be able to swing it in a proper manner in order to capitalize on the features of the club as well as your own physical attributes.

Improving Your Overall Game

Once the key elements of your swing are identified, specific strength and flexibility exercises can then be prescribed. The point of these exercises is to duplicate each distinct action that takes place in the swing. Strength and flexibility are developed by repeating the same movement pattern through the same range of motion and with the same type of muscular contraction seen in the swing. In this way, the abilities that you gain from completing the exercises will have an immediate and direct effect on your swing. Usually it takes only three or four exercise sessions—a few days to a week—to see major changes!

It is well established in the scientific literature that the hips should initiate the downswing since the hips are the area in which the center of gravity is located (the point where all the body weight is concentrated). Thus, when you move the center of gravity, you initiate movement of the entire body. Movement of the legs follows naturally to maintain weight balance over the feet.

The muscles that are involved in sliding (shifting) the hips forward are located on the side of the hips; thus, a hip exercise involving the same muscles in the same range of motion is needed to strengthen these muscles in the precise manner in which they are used in the weight shift. As a result, you learn to better execute this action, which in turn enables you to achieve more effective hip and shoulder rotation. The increased levels of strength, flexibility, and speed allow you more control of the club pathway, therefore increasing the amount of power and accuracy that you apply to the ball.

By closely examining each key action of the total swing, you will not only improve your understanding of each movement, but you will see how the specialized strength and flexibility exercises can improve each of these actions. It's not difficult to realize that this strategy can quickly produce improvement in your total game.

Getting Started

Unfortunately, it takes an injury before most individuals begin to see the true value of doing specific exercises. One of my students provides a classic example of this. This individual was in a severe car accident that required him to undergo multiple shoulder surgeries. Most of the muscle mass in his shoulder was lost as a result, so he was on a rehabilitation program to build up the remaining muscle mass.

I helped him by prescribing various exercises for the shoulder. I introduced specialized exercises designed to help him swing the golf club properly. At first he was a nonbeliever; that is to say, he only did the shoulder exercises. As he began to see positive results, however, he slowly came around and soon incorporated the golf exercises into his routine. It wasn't long before he experienced some dramatic improvements in his golf game. Not only were his shots going farther, but he gained consistency and confidence as a player.

He continued his exercises for about four or five months, and before long developed into a great long-ball hitter. This individual is firmly convinced that the exercises played a major role not only in his recovery, but in the overall improvement of his game. He now has many of his pupils doing these same exercises. He is a firm advocate who came to realize that it is only through proper physical training that a golfer can realize his or her true potential.

Develop an Understanding

In the following chapters you will see photographs printed directly from high shutter-speed digital videotapes of professional golfers. After each key action of the swing, a specialized strength and flexibility exercise is presented that duplicates the key action involved. Photos of the exercises are also included so that you, too, can clearly understand and duplicate each exercise.

By studying the combination of swing action illustrations and specialized exercises, you will gain a better understanding of how each of these exercises relates to your own personal swing. If your swing deviates greatly from the norm on the actions presented, then you should modify some of the exercises to fit your swing. Or, you may find it more advantageous to modify and improve your swing by undertaking specific exercises. Just keep this thought in mind: completing these simple exercises on a weekly basis will give you the necessary strength and flexibility required to execute the proper mechanics of the golf swing and will help you develop the muscular feel necessary to reach your potential.

2

Key Physical Qualities
Strength and Flexibility

The Importance of Strength and Flexibility

Strength and flexibility are the most important physical qualities necessary for golfers because they are both closely related to the key aspects of the swing. The golfer must develop a combination of strength and flexibility in order to improve these key elements of the golf swing:

- Maintain a stable stance
- Maintain a safe back position
- Demonstrate active flexibility
- Increase clubhead speed
- Control body movements
- Develop a muscular feel for the swing
- Effectively learn the golf swing
- Modify swing technique
- Prevent injury
- Develop strength endurance
- Speed up rehabilitation after injury
- Improve breathing technique
- Improve aerobic capabilities
- Slow down effects of the aging process

The main outcome of a specialized strength and flexibility exercise program is improvement in your ability to swing the golf club in the most efficient manner to ensure maximum distance and accuracy. Believe it or not, specialized strength and flexibility exercises can enhance and improve your swing in a shorter period of time than if you doubled your playing time! Specifically, greater strength and flexibility will enable you to perform the key elements of the golf swing with less difficulty.

Key Elements of the Golf Swing
Maintain a Stable Stance

When you strengthen the leg, hip, and lower back muscles, you become better able to hold a stable basic stance throughout the entire swing. This enables you to have a more powerful swing together with greater accuracy. It also increases your ability to control body movements when executing all shots, particularly when you find yourself in uncommon playing positions (for example, in a situation where most of your weight must be placed on one leg).

Maintain a Safe Back Position

One of the main reasons a player might suffer a lower back injury results from having a rounded back (spine) in the basic stance and during the swing. By strengthening the lower back and hip extensor muscles, you can maintain the trunk position with its normal spinal curvature during the entire swing. In this position, the forces acting on the discs are greatly reduced. This, in turn, allows you to swing safely with as much force as you desire and is likely to result in more accurate and consistent ball striking.

Demonstrate Active Flexibility

Golfers are often advised to do static stretches in which they hold a position for approximately thirty seconds. Although such stretching is often recommended to prevent injury, studies have shown that the number of injuries is generally the same regardless of whether one does such stretches. Contrary to popular belief, it has never been proven that static stretches prevent injury!

To ensure a full swing, your joints must have an adequate range of motion. At the same time, your muscles must provide maximum joint stability throughout the range of motion—especially in the follow-through. To achieve this, you need not only strong muscles, but strong ligaments and tendons, which also prevent the joints from going beyond their range of motion. If you have unstable joints—a situation that occurs when the ligaments and tendons are overstretched (as often occurs in static stretching) and the muscles are not strong enough to maintain joint integrity—you are highly prone to injury.

Golf is dynamic, not static. For this reason, doing static stretches to achieve greater flexibility is not specific to the golf swing. To make your stretches more functional, you must do active stretches that prepare the muscles for action and enable you to develop flexibility with strength. Keep in mind that it is the strength of the muscles that must move the limbs and trunk through the range of motion needed in the swing. Having great flexibility does not guarantee or have any relation whatsoever to the ability of the muscles to move the trunk or limbs through a certain range of motion.

To increase range of motion, you must not only develop greater flexibility, but you must also develop strength throughout the new range of motion. In the exercises presented in this book, you will learn to develop strength and flexibility within the same exercise. This is very specific to the golf swing and is a natural way to stretch and strengthen the muscles and joints. It is also the most efficient method to effect positive changes in your swing in the shortest amount of time.

Increase Clubhead Speed

When you increase the strength of the muscles involved in the swing, you can move the trunk and arms faster, more forcefully, and with a higher degree of coordination. As a result, you will be able to generate more clubhead speed to produce increased force on impact and ultimately achieve greater hitting distance with your swing. Studies show that professional golfers execute the entire swing faster (by about 0.2–0.3 seconds) than average golfers. Because strength is related to speed of movement, the greater your strength levels, the faster and more forcefully you can move the hips, shoulders, and arms.

For example, by increasing the strength of the rotary muscles of the midsection—the muscle group that rotates the shoulders in the downswing—you can easily gain an additional 40 to 50 yards on your drives. By doing specialized strength and flexibility exercises for the hip, shoulder, arm, and wrist actions, golfers with good coordination can easily and consistently drive the ball 250 to 300 yards with accuracy!

Control Body Movements

Control of body movements is related to neuromuscular coordination, which is the key to an effective golf swing. Swing technique involves an integration of the nervous and muscular systems to control the movements. Part of neuromuscular coordination is muscle strength—not necessarily maximum strength, but sufficient strength to enable the movements to be executed safely, effectively, and explosively. Understand that coordination consists of contracting the muscles with the necessary intensity, with the right timing, and in the correct sequence. Thus, by doing the recommended specialized strength exercises, you can enhance coordination.

Develop Muscular Feel for the Swing

Most golfers who have played for any length of time are familiar with what can best be described as a *muscular feel* for the club and swing. This muscular feel is a key factor in learning to groove your shots. If you need improvement in a key action of the swing, then you must practice the particular movement to get the neuromuscular pathway (muscular feel) developed.

By repeatedly doing a strength exercise that duplicates a specific action, you not only learn the feel of the movement, but you also increase control of the movement. As a result, it is much easier to incorporate the new or modified action into the overall swing. Once this action is mastered, you will soon develop a feel for it.

For example, I have worked with many golfers who have difficulty separating hip rotation from shoulder rotation in the downswing. By doing specialized exercises—in this case, executing reverse trunk twists and hip rotation using rubber tubing to pull the hips around before the shoulders—the problem is easily corrected. Soon you learn the feel of early hip rotation, enabling you to not only achieve a larger X-factor (separation between the hips and shoulders), but also to create greater power during the shoulder turn.

Effectively Learn the Golf Swing

The necessity of strength in learning the golf swing or key swing actions is evident when first attempting new movements. For example, you need strong lower back muscles to hold your back in position (in its neutral curvature). You need adequate strength of the wrist muscles to hold the club in a cocked position, and leg strength to maintain a stable lower-body position during the swing. If you do not have the strength to carry out these functions, you cannot learn to execute the specific actions that an effective swing demands. As a result, you may develop a poor or even potentially dangerous swing. Remember, the swing you develop is determined by your physical capabilities.

Modify Swing Technique

The two basic ways to achieve a better golf swing are improving your physical capabilities, as we have previously discussed, and improving your technique. If your instructor recommends a particular change in technique and you do not have the physical ability to make the change, you will not be able to incorporate the suggestion to improve your swing. For example, if you do not have sufficient midsection strength and flexibility, you will be unable to separate hip rotation from shoulder rotation and you will not be capable of generating more force in shoulder rotation. By adopting specialized exercises, however, it is possible to develop the ability to execute these key actions which in turn produce greater clubhead speed.

After I identify a golfer's weak points, I suggest special exercises that duplicate the specific action in need of improvement. The golfer then develops the ability to modify the technique to make the swing more effective. Some very simple exercises have allowed these golfers to increase their driving distances substantially while achieving greater accuracy. The exercises have also served to improve consistency in overall shot production.

I can relate many examples showing how specific exercises can enable you to achieve the modifications desired, but suffice it to say that the development of your physical abilities—especially strength and flexibility—plays the critical role in not only shaping your swing, but in hitting the ball farther and with greater accuracy. Let me again emphasize the point—your swing is determined by your physical capabilities!

Prevent Injury

Adequate strength and flexibility of the muscles and joints, together with effective technique, can also help prevent injury. Well-stabilized limbs and joints that are under control when the swing forces are encountered greatly reduce the potential for injury. In such cases, muscles can safely withstand the forces that act against them. If your body movements are uncoordinated or uncontrolled when you execute the swing, however, the muscles, tendons, and ligaments have little margin for error. As a result, they are much more likely to become stretched or torn.

The movements involved in the golf swing demand considerable skill. To hit the ball far, you must produce the maximum range of motion and force in the joints involved, especially in the hips, back (spine), and shoulders. It should come as no surprise that these are the areas in which you are particularly vulnerable to injury. Just remain mindful that adequate levels of strength and flexibility coupled with good technique will not only greatly decrease the possibility of injury, but will also enhance the quality of your game.

If you are generally healthy and able to play a round of golf without any significant physical problems, injury prevention may not seem important to you. However, I am confident that you are aware of the many players (including professional players on the regular or senior tours) who suffer from joint or muscle plain or who have experienced injuries while swinging a club. You probably even know some golfers who can no longer play at all because of injuries sustained while playing.

Let's look at some statistics. According to the 1995 Consumer Products Safety Commission, there were 39,928 golf injuries treated in emergency rooms. When you add the number of injuries that were self-treated or that required a visit to the family physician, this number could easily be quadrupled. This does not take into consideration the number of chronic problems that golfers learn to "live with" in order to keep playing the sport.

The point is that almost all golfers experience some physical problems throughout their playing years, especially in the lower back, followed by the shoulders and elbows. Very often these injuries are due to overplaying, which often results from the general recommendation that to become a better player, one must play more frequently. It is important to realize that increasing your playing (or hitting) time may lead to overuse injuries, wear and tear that results when your body cannot handle the continual stress placed upon the muscles and joints.

Just because your scores improve from extra playing or hitting does not mean that you are also improving in terms of strength, flexibility, and muscular endurance. The result is usually the opposite! The advice is simple—avoid preventable injuries that come about when your strength level cannot handle built-up joint and muscle stress.

Develop Strength Endurance

Strength endurance, the ability to repeat movements requiring strength, is necessary for preventing the onset of fatigue. You must be able to execute the same swing with the same effectiveness on the 18th hole as you do on the 1st hole in order to achieve success. Strength endurance is the quality that allows you to maintain a consistent and effective swing with less energy expenditure.

Strength by itself is important for each individual swing. But because most golfers execute 100 or more swings during the course of playing a round, it is also necessary to develop strength endurance in order to consistently execute effective and efficient swings. Even walking to the ball from hole to hole can be less tiring. In addition, when you are able to repeat your best swing a greater percentage of the time, you are less likely to become injured.

Speed Up Rehabilitation After Injury

In the event of an injury, increased strength levels aid in the rehabilitation process and speed up recovery time, so it's hardly surprising that strength training is one of the primary methods used in rehabilitation of injuries. Muscular activity as an aid in medical restoration lies in the development of strength, endurance, flexibility, skill, and relaxation. These elements are basic to successful recovery, as well as to playing good golf.

Improve Breathing Technique

Breathing technique plays an important role in executing the golf swing, relaxing on shots, and walking the course—especially a hilly one. When the respiratory muscles are strong, you are capable of taking in and processing more air per breath. As a result, you can process greater amounts of oxygen. The body needs higher levels of oxygen not only for the production of energy, but also to help in recovery time following exertion.

The stronger your respiratory muscles are, the more effective your cardiovascular endurance. By improving the strength of the muscles involved in breathing, you will be able to recover faster after each hole, maintain higher energy levels when walking the course, and prevent the premature onset of fatigue.

For example, let's look at relaxation—it is based on your ability to relax the muscles. When you are tense, the muscles are under contraction and don't allow you to execute movements smoothly or in a coordinated fashion. When you develop the ability to properly contract and relax the muscles, however, you will again be on your way to achieving a more effective swing.

Improve Aerobic Capabilities

Strength is closely related to the development of aerobic capabilities—efficient functioning of the cardiovascular and respiratory systems. There is no doubt that improving your aerobic abilities will enhance your overall playing skill by preventing undue fatigue when walking the course. As a result, you will feel better when executing your shots. Too often, *aerobic training*—sometimes known as *general conditioning*—is erroneously considered the best way to prepare yourself physically for playing golf.

As you engage in aerobic training (activities such as running, cycling, swimming, rowing, or general cyclical and continuous activity), your cardiorespiratory functions improve. Keep in mind, however, that strength does not increase! Remember to develop strength along with aerobic endurance. Improvements in muscle strength will actually enable you to do aerobic activities with greater ease and with less risk of injury.

Slow Down Effects of the Aging Process

Strength training is especially beneficial in slowing the effects of the aging process. Many golfers are already in middle age or older and anticipate playing as long as possible. In order to do this, however, they need adequate levels of strength, flexibility, and other physical abilities. Most individuals lose strength as they age, but the main reason for this is simple—they do not do supplementary strength training exercises to maintain the fitness levels present in youth.

Remember, it is never too late to gain strength. It is a fact that individuals in their 70s and 80s are capable of doubling their strength within a matter of weeks! By maintaining or increasing levels of strength and other physical qualities, you will not experience or be aware of the drastic changes typically associated with aging. You will not stop the changes, but you will forestall them.

While analyzing senior golfers (including tour players), I have found that most have lost a great deal of flexibility—especially in the midsection, which plays an especially important role in generating power in the swing. As a result, some pros advocate a step forward in the swing to ensure weight shift and adequate force. This change in swing technique shows how these golfers have lost the strength of the hip muscles as well as the flexibility and balance needed to maintain a stable position. But a step forward would not be necessary if a few simple exercises were done to maintain or improve strength and flexibility.

Many golfers can play the game fairly well, mainly due to a degree of consistency developed through years of practice. In spite of physical losses, these golfers are still capable of executing consistent (but not always powerful) swings. However, as you begin to lose more of the physical qualities, injuries become more prevalent and erratic shots increase. Thus, it is extremely important—especially for senior golfers—to maintain or increase strength, flexibility, balance, and coordination in order to preserve the level of quality in their game.

Specialized Exercises
Strength and Flexibility

General Versus Specialized Physical Exercises

All exercises are not created equal. Even when two exercises involve the same muscles, they can be substantially different. For example, one exercise may work a group of muscles with greater intensity at the start of the initial movement, while another exercise may not bring the same muscle group into play until midrange. Some muscles have multiple actions, and therefore one exercise may involve a specific action while others focus on different actions. Thus, before going into the strength and flexibility exercises that are specific to golf, it is important to differentiate between general and specialized physical exercises.

General exercises are those exercises that are not directly related to the specific actions of the golf swing. These activities are used for overall body conditioning—strengthening basic muscle groups to increase your functional potential.

The push-up exercise can be used to illustrate the concept of a general strength exercise. Here we have a common exercise executed by golfers and fitness buffs in which the arms extend on either side of the body and move forward and backward in relation to the shoulders.

In the golf swing, however, the arms move in a diagonal pattern in relation to the trunk. Thus, the push-up may be a good exercise for strengthening the shoulders and arms, but it is not directly related to a golf swing movement.

If you have weak shoulders, the push-up exercise can improve your strength capabilities. Although this may indirectly help your game, understand that it is not as effective as an exercise in which arm and shoulder movements duplicate the exact pathway of a golf swing. This would be known as a *specialized exercise.* An example of a specialized exercise would involve pulling your arms down and across the body against resistance in the same pathway and in the same range of motion as in the golf swing.

Criteria for Specialized Exercises

The key to improving the swing is to do specialized exercises that duplicate swing movements and actions. In this way, the development of the physical abilities that are specific to the swing will have the greatest impact on improving your ability to swing the club well and to have greater success in your golf game. The general criteria for specialized exercises are as follows:

1. The exercise must duplicate the exact movement witnessed in certain actions of the overall swing. For example, there is an exercise to duplicate the exact wrist, arm, and shoulder actions.

2. Each exercise must involve the same type of muscular contraction that is used in the actual swing. For example, in the downswing the muscles undergo a powerful shortening contraction (after initially being tensed) to produce the force and resulting clubhead speed. In the follow-through, most of the muscles undergo a strong muscle lengthening contraction to slow down and stop the club before an injury can occur. The specialized exercises can also duplicate the speed of movement. Holding a stable stance requires static contractions so that there is no movement.

3. The specialized exercises must have the same range of motion as that used in your actual swing. For example, to improve the arm action in the downswing, doing an exercise with your arm directly above your head and then pulling it downward to the side does not duplicate the same range of muscular arm action present in the swing (even though it uses the same muscles). More specific is to move the arm down and simultaneously across the body in order to duplicate what realistically occurs in the swing.

Developing Specialized Exercises

The concept of exercise specificity is new to golf, but the term *specificity* is not. Many authors have used the term *specific golf exercises,* but few (if any) actually satisfy the aforementioned criteria. The specificity described by these authors usually refers to strengthening or stretching the muscles that may be involved, but not in the way that they are used in the actual swing.

For example, there are strength training programs out there that claim to be sport specific. I have come across a number of them in magazines, most claiming to be strength training programs specifically for golf. I have then found that some of these same programs are featured in other magazines—one for runners, another for tennis players—claiming to be specific to those sports as well. The problem here is that the exercises in these magazines were identical. The programs were not sport specific at all. In essence, these were general training programs, total-body conditioning exercises that involved most of the major muscles of the body. According to these authors, executing all of the exercises involving the major muscles of the body is a satisfactory means of exercising the muscles involved in your particular sport. As I have previously explained, this is simply not true and is far from the exercise specificity that will help you find improvement in your golf game.

Typical golf strength and conditioning programs deal with general exercises to get you "in shape." In some cases, the prescribed exercises involve the same muscles that are used in the golf swing. But if these exercises do not duplicate the same range of motion, the same type of muscle contraction, or the exact movement coordination that takes place in the swing, they will not be completely functional because they will not be used directly in the swing.

For example, researchers who have done electromyographic (EMG) studies to determine the muscular involvement in the golf swing have found that the abdominals play a major role. To strengthen the abdominals, the researchers recommended the crunch and the crunch with a twist. These exercises do, of course, strengthen the abdominals, but only through a very small range of motion that is not specific to the swing.

More specifically, when the abdominals come into play, it is mainly the abdominal oblique muscles that rotate the shoulders in the downswing and follow-through. The obliques also play a major role in midsection flexibility—especially in the separation between hip and shoulder rotation, a range of action that can be more than 90 degrees.

In the crunch (or sit-up) exercise, it is mainly the rectus abdominis that is strengthened. The crunch with a twist involves the obliques, but the range of motion is extremely small—and, more importantly, the twisting occurs when the spine is flexed. This is a potentially dangerous situation, as rotation of the trunk should always take place when the spine is maintained in its normal curvature position. Thus, even though the exercises strengthen the abdominals, they are not specific to the swing or to the actual muscle action involved.

Consider the wrist curl (wrist flexion) and reverse wrist curl (wrist extension and hyperextension) exercises, which are commonly used to strengthen the wrists. There is no doubt that the wrists will get stronger from doing these exercises, but you should recognize that these actions are not used in the swing (unless you scoop the ball). The muscles involved must be strong to block the wrists and limit their flexion and extension action during contact.

The wrist cocking that produces a longer backswing and the uncocking that produces the greatest power in the downswing consist of radial and ulnar flexion, respectively. In the backswing there is radial flexion, in which the hands stay in line with the forearms and the thumb sides of the hands move toward the forearm in order to cock the wrists. In the downswing there is ulnar flexion, in which the pinkie sides of the hands move toward the forearm in order to "break" the wrists.

After the ulnar flexion there is supination and pronation (rolling) of the hands and rotation of the arms in order to ensure square contact of the clubhead on the ball. The point here is that you should do exercises that duplicate these more specific actions, not just wrist flexion and extension.

Developing Physical and Psychological Qualities

Specialized strength exercises are used to develop physical and psychological qualities that apply directly to the golf swing. These exercises are designed and selected so that the movements and actions closely match those seen in the golf swing.

Specialized exercises can take the form of imitation exercises—a type of exercise used for instruction as well as for improving the actual swing. In such exercises, you closely match the neuromuscular coordination involved in the swing or in some portion of the swing. The imitation is completed by imagining that you are performing the movements under realistic conditions. Posing in front of a mirror and then carrying out the various movements of the swing would be one way in which to execute an imitation exercise.

Performing specialized exercises promotes the development of psychological traits such as decisiveness, willpower, perseverance, and confidence. You exhibit these traits when performing specialized exercises because they involve concentration and psychological qualities similar to those present when hitting the ball and during competitive play.

The execution of some specialized exercises requires ultimate concentration and perseverance in order to develop the appropriate neuromuscular pathway (muscular feel). For the specialized exercise to have maximum positive transfer, you must be decisive in your movements and actions in order to develop the confidence to be able to repeat the swing action during play.

Proper Breathing During Specialized Exercises

When you begin your exercises, how you breathe isn't terribly critical. As you increase the resistance, however, how you breathe is very important. Because of this, you should develop proper breathing patterns from the start. This also applies to the golf swing.

The instructions for the exercises tell you to inhale and hold your breath on the exertion—that is, on the hardest part of the exercise, when you are overcoming the resistance. You then exhale on the return, staying in control of the movements. But don't be surprised if you read or hear the opposite from other sources—that you should exhale on exertion and inhale on return.

The widely used recommendation to exhale on exertion is based on theory, not research, and applies mainly to people with heart and circulatory system problems. For example, if you hold your breath for too long (up to eight seconds with a maximal exertion), you could pass out. That is because the internal pressure in the chest and abdomen increases when you hold your breath on exertion. If it increases greatly, it squeezes down on the blood vessels shuttling blood and oxygen to and from the heart. When this happens, you can black out (but rarely, and only on maximum exertion).

If you are without cardiovascular problems and do not hold your breath for more than a few seconds as needed in the recommended exercises, the breath-holding on exertion is perfectly safe. It makes the exercises safer and more effective. If you have high blood pressure or other circulatory system or heart problems, avoid heavy resistance and breath-holding.

Inhaling and holding the breath briefly on exertion—any exertion, in all sports, including golf—comes naturally. Many studies have shown that whenever athletic skills are executed properly, athletes hold their breath on the exertion—during the power phase, when maximum force is generated. The breath-holding is especially important in the golf swing, not only for greater distance but for accuracy.

Inhaling and holding the breath on exertion provides up to 20 percent greater force, stabilizes the spine, and helps prevent lower back injuries. It transforms the trunk (and, in fact, the whole body) into a stable unit against which your hips, shoulders, and arms can move effectively.

Breathing exercises can also help you to relax. For example, it is not uncommon to read that you should inhale and then exhale before executing the swing. This is a good technique to help you relax. But before starting the swing, it is important that the muscles have some tension—not excessive tension, but sufficient tension to execute the swing as needed.

Thus, inhalation and breath-holding are needed immediately before and during execution of the swing. Studies done with devices to monitor breathing patterns have proven this beyond any doubt. To execute the best swing, you must hold your breath during execution of the swing!

In effective breathing, do not take a maximal breath and then hold it. Doing this can make you very uncomfortable. Just take a breath slightly greater than usual and then hold it to experience the positive benefits. This is especially important for stabilizing the body, holding the spine in position, and getting greater power in your shots. The entire swing is completed very quickly. Thus, you should have no fear of holding the breath too long or of overexerting yourself.

The idea that breath-holding is needed when doing heavy lifting can also be inferred from the recommendations given for relaxation. In order to relax, you are told to inhale and then exhale. As you exhale you relax the muscles. In essence, exhalation is associated with relaxation. Is it therefore wise to exhale when you are lifting a heavy weight—when you need maximum control of the weight not only for safety purposes but also to do the exercise correctly and effectively? Your natural instinct is to hold your breath when lifting heavy weights. Simply watch someone in the gym lifting a heavy weight and you will see that the breath is held during the exertion. Some visible signs are puffed out cheeks, distention of the blood vessels, a closed mouth. Danger is present only if the breath is held too long—two or more times the amount of time taken to do an exercise at a normal, moderate rate of speed.

Using Exercise Equipment to Achieve Specific Results

The discussion of specificity of exercise would not be complete without a mention of some of the exercise machines that are presently being used for improving strength. The companies that make these machines make many claims that often do not hold up under close scrutiny.

For example, some of the machines create excessive resistance, which interferes with coordination. Most do not duplicate the muscle action or the range of motion present in the golf swing. On many of the exercise machines, the movement is guided. You must do what the machine dictates rather than having the benefit of the machine offering you resistance so that you can move in a manner specific enough to duplicate the golf swing and to execute safe movements. Most exercise machines, for instance, have upward and downward movements; yet the golf swing is mostly rotational, using the diagonal movements of the limbs. Because of this, most machines do not duplicate what occurs in the golf swing.

There are, however, some specific pieces of equipment that do simulate what occurs in the golf swing. Some of these machines have value for development of particular muscles. In general, they are all good for overall strengthening. Just remember—if the movement is not the same as it is in the actual golf swing, then the exercise is not specific.

It should also be noted that many exercise machines can lead to injury if they cannot be properly adjusted to fit different-sized individuals. Most machines are made for the hypothetical "average" individual. If you deviate from this norm, the resulting movements may be dangerous to your joints. In addition, exercise machines do not improve balance, a very important physical quality needed by golfers. Without adequate balance, a full, smooth swing is impossible to achieve. For these reasons, free weights and elastic cords with which your body and limbs can move freely are much more effective.

Care should also be taken with the use of weighted donuts that are placed at the end of the golf club to increase clubhead speed. The concept of using heavier and lighter weights is valid, and, when used properly, can greatly improve your swing speed. However, if the weight is excessive (even if only by ounces), it changes the neuromuscular coordination that you have developed over the years and can cause injury.

To my knowledge there have been no studies completed that determine how much weight can be used on the clubhead before golf swing technique changes. Studies that have focused on other sports, such as the shot put, found that even less than a pound of weight can substantially change technique execution. Thus, if you want to use a donut, be sure that it does not change how you swing. If you use a heavy donut to loosen up before playing, you should do it well before you start playing.

In addition, you should take regular swings to "re-groove" the neuromuscular pathway before you begin to play. Use of a weighted donut has been popularized in baseball. However, it has been shown quite conclusively that the use of such donuts, even though they may give the players the feeling of having a very light, quick swing, actually changes swing technique. The players insist that they can swing faster, which is probably true, but not in the same way in which they are accustomed! As a result, they usually end up with more strikeouts.

When you swing a club with a weight attached close to the end of the club, and then execute the swing, the momentum (force) generated can be very high. As a result it can cause injury, especially when trying to stop the fast-moving weight in the follow-through. The momentum can also carry the club through a swing plane that differs from your pre-grooved pathway.

The development of strength must be in synchronization with your swing for maximum effectiveness. This is considered usable strength—the strength that you gain is displayed in your swing. This represents the greatest value that specialized exercises can give you that general exercises cannot.

Because of the need for skill duplication, most exercises are best done with elastic cords and free weights. Hip and shoulder rotation exercises are most effectively executed with rubber tubing, such as Active Cords, and medicine balls. The reason for this is that it is very difficult—in some cases impossible—to duplicate the exact rotational movements of the hips and shoulders with dumbbells, barbells, or machines. The free weights—consisting mainly of dumbbells and specialized equipment such as the Strength Bar and Exer Rings—are necessary for addressing the finer, more precise movements specific to golf.

CHAPTER
4

The Stance
Stable and Dynamic

Effective Stance and Posture

The golf stance refers to not only your body position when addressing the ball, but also to your body position during the swing. When hitting the ball on nonlevel surfaces, on different types of terrain, under tree branches, and when in heavy rough, you must usually make modifications in the swing. As a result, your stance must change to accommodate the situation. The initial stance is very important, but body posture during the swing is even more critical for ensuring an effective swing and for preventing the onset of injury, especially to the spine.

For example, picture yourself in a position with the ball about a foot lower than your feet. In this case, rather than bending the knees to get low, which prevents you from shifting or rotating the hips, you should bend over from the hips. With ample hip joint flexibility and strength, you can get the trunk almost horizontal while holding the normal spinal curvature. This allows you to rotate the shoulders and swing the club to produce an effective hit.

Being able to maintain a stable position during execution of the swing is a key element in having smooth, well-coordinated body actions. When you are capable of holding the legs, hips, and trunk in position (both statically and dynamically) as you execute the swing, not only will excessive up-and-down and side-to-side actions be eliminated, but you will hit with maximum force through the ball.

Developing a Stable Body Position

A stable body position enables you to execute fuller and more effective hip and shoulder rotation not only in the backswing, but also in the downswing and follow-through. For many golfers, maintaining a stable position, especially a stable spine position, is the key to the prevention of back problems.

For example, if you maintain the normal spinal curvature (a slightly arched spine in the lumbar area of the lower back) when you rotate the hips and shoulders, the movement is perfectly safe. If, however, you rotate the hips or shoulders with a rounded spine or fail to clear (shift and rotate) the hips before the shoulder rotation in the downswing, the chances of injury to the spine are greatly increased.

Thus, the key to an effective and dynamic swing is to maintain the lower body and trunk in a stable position. To do this, it is necessary to have strong muscles in the legs, hips, and lower back. The stronger these muscles are, the easier it is to hold a relatively relaxed stance. Such a stance allows explosive movements to be made safely, especially for the lower back.

Exercises

The following three exercises can greatly improve the effectiveness of your stance and produce positive results in your golf swing.

- Basic squat
- Delay squat
- Good morning

The basic squat and delay squat exercises strengthen mainly the quadriceps muscles on the anterior (front) thigh. Their main function is to maintain the knees in a slightly bent position during the initial stance and during the swing. They also improve your ability to walk the course, especially a hilly one.

The good morning exercise duplicates the trunk and hip position in the stance. At the same time, it strengthens the lower back muscles and stretches and strengthens the hamstring muscles on the rear of the thighs.

Joint Action: Knee Bend for Lower-Body Stability

To maintain a stable lower body during all phases of the swing, it is important that you have relatively strong quadriceps muscles. These muscles play a major role in maintaining the hips on the same level during the weight shift and hip rotation. In addition, they hold the legs steady during the hip and shoulder rotation and arm action. When the quadriceps muscles are weak, it is possible to see straightening and bending of the knees during the swing, which in turn leads to poor ball contact and the pos-

Figure 4.1   Front view of basic stance

sibility of knee injury during trunk rotation. Also, if the right leg is not stable during the backswing, excessive backward hip (weight) shift can occur.

To hold the knees and hips level during the swing, there is also a degree of ankle and hip joint flexion. In essence, all three leg joints are involved in maintaining the body in a balanced position with the weight lowered and centered over the feet. However, the knees play the predominant role. Examine the golf stance from different views (see figs. 4.1–4.3). Note the level positioning of the knees and hips and the incline of the trunk.

Basic Squat

The basic squat and delay squat are the best exercises for strengthening the muscles involved in assuming and maintaining an effective and stable golf stance. The squat was once widely condemned as being dangerous to the knees. However, the overwhelming

Figure 4.2   Side view of basic stance

Figure 4.3   Knees and hips are level, the trunk is inclined.

modern consensus is that this exercise is far superior to any other for the purpose of strengthening the quadriceps muscles and preventing injury to the knees. As an extra bonus, learning to do the squat correctly can help a golfer when lifting the golf bag, as well as when lifting any object (especially a heavy one).

In order to learn proper technique in the initial stages of this exercise, do not use any external resistance. To execute the squat, assume a standing position with your arms relaxed at your sides (fig. 4.4a). Lock the lower back in place so that you maintain the natural curvature of the spine. When ready, inhale and hold your breath as you lower your body into a squat. Keep the feet flat on the ground and the lower back slightly arched. When you lower the upper body, move the hips to the rear and down as the trunk inclines forward (fig. 4.4b). Look directly in front at all times.

Lower yourself until your thighs are nearly parallel to the ground; however, do this only if you can still maintain proper trunk and spine position and can

keep your feet flat on the ground. If you begin to round your back or if your heels rise, stop the exercise immediately and do not go any lower. Remember, rounding the lower back, especially when holding weights on the shoulders or in the hands, can be dangerous to the lower back. Raising the heels, which moves the knees out beyond the front of the feet in the down position, can result in injury to the knees.

After reaching the lower position, straighten the legs and raise the trunk to reassume the erect standing position and exhale. In the squat, the legs should do all the work while the lower back muscles remain under static contraction to hold the proper spinal position. Doing this will improve your ability to hold your spine in position in the initial stance and during the swing.

If you need greater balance, raise the arms in front to shoulder level as you lower the body, and lower the arms as you rise up. For greater resistance, hold dumbbells in the hands or use rubber tubing.

(a)

Figure 4.4 The basic squat starting position

(b)

Keep the feet flat and the lower spine slightly arched.

Variation—Rubber Tubing Squat

To execute the squat with rubber tubing, assume a standing position with the tubing under the feet, holding onto one end of the tubing in each hand (see figs. 4.5a–b). In the erect standing position, there should be strong tension on the tubing. In some cases you should wrap the tubing around each foot as you stand on it to shorten the length in order to get more tension. Execute the squat as just described.

Delay Squat

The regular squat is very effective for strengthening the muscles through a full range of motion. However, during the swing the leg muscles must remain under isometric contraction to hold a steady stance position. Thus, it is necessary to develop the muscles as they are involved in lowering the body and in maintaining the static posture. For this, the delay squat is most effective.

To execute, assume a standing position with the feet shoulder-width apart (see fig. 4.6a). Then very slowly begin to lower the body for four one-second counts. As you slowly lower the body, move the hips slightly to the rear and incline the trunk slightly forward. You should lower the body approximately 2 to 3 inches in four seconds, after which you hold the static contraction position for another four seconds (see fig. 4.6b). Then, once again begin to slowly lower the body for four counts, and hold the position for four counts (see fig. 4.6c). Next, slowly lower the body for a third time. Upon reaching the bottom position (see fig. 4.6d), hold again for four seconds and then jump up for more resilient legs (see fig. 4.6e).

When doing the delay squat, it is important that the down movement be done very slowly. This

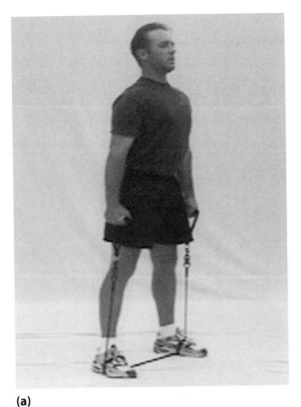

(a)

Figure 4.5 Rubber tubing squat starting position

(b)

As for the basic squat, move the hips to the rear and down while the trunk inclines forward.

ensures adequate development of eccentric strength, which is used to lower the body under control. The isometric (static) strength is developed when you hold the legs and body in position for four counts. If you find your legs beginning to shake as you do the exercise, stop immediately, as the leg muscles are now becoming overloaded.

Although this appears to be an easy exercise, it can prove to be quite difficult. Because of this, do not attempt many repetitions initially, and gradually build up to five full repetitions for one set. Use dumbbells or Active Cords for greater resistance.

Joint Action: Hip Flexion with Proper Trunk Position

The ability to hold the proper trunk position is developed to some degree when doing the squat. However, it requires special work to emphasize holding the proper spinal curvature in the initial stance

as well as during the swing. If you look closely at the side view pictures of the golfer's stance (see figs. 4.2–4.3), you can see how the back should maintain its normal curvature—a straight or slightly arched lower spine. There is basically a straight line that can be drawn from the mid-back through the hip joints.

Good Morning

The good morning exercise is one of the best exercises that you can do to strengthen the hip extensor muscles (gluteus maximus and hamstrings) that are responsible for holding the trunk in a forward lean. In addition, this exercise strengthens the erector spinae muscles of the lower back, which are responsible for maintaining the proper and safe curvature of the spine. When you have the correct curvature of the spine, hip and shoulder (trunk) rotation can take place safely and effectively. Trunk rotation with a rounded or hyperextended spine can be dangerous!

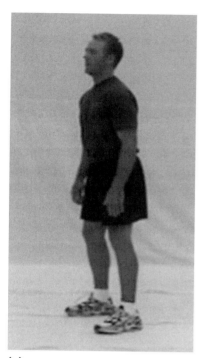

(a)

Figure 4.6 Delay squat starting position

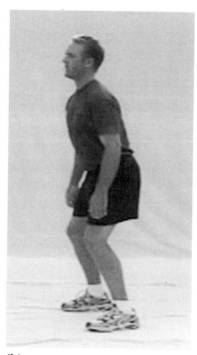

(b)

Lower slowly and hold four counts.

(c)

Lower farther and hold.

(d)

Lower again and hold.

(e)

Jump up for resilient legs.

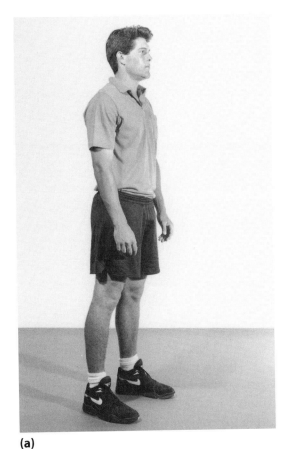

(a)

Figure 4.7 Good morning starting position

(b)

Bend from the hips, maintaining effective spinal curvature.

This exercise appears easy, but in reality, it is difficult for most golfers, even experienced and professional golfers. The reason for this is that most people are accustomed to bending over from the waist with a rounded spine rather than bending over from the hips. In analyzing professional, amateur, and recreational golfers, I can safely say that at least one third to one half of all golfers assume a rounded spine in the initial stance. For many of them, this leads to lower back problems.

By doing the good morning exercise on a regular basis, you can soon develop the strength and flexibility needed to hold an effective stance and to eliminate problems that arise from the rounded spine position. This exercise will also develop the muscular feel and the strength and flexibility needed to maintain a good trunk position.

When learning the good morning exercise, use only the resistance of your upper body. Assume an erect standing position and lock the lower back in its normal, slightly arched spinal position (see fig. 4.7a). When ready, inhale and hold your breath as you bend over from the hips, maintaining the effective spinal curvature (see fig. 4.7b). Keep the legs straight in order to get a good stretch of the hamstrings as you bend over. If you experience any stress in the knees (for example, if they hyperextend), then bend the knees slightly and hold the legs slightly bent during execution.

As you incline the trunk forward from the hips, push the pelvis to the rear to keep the body in balance. Note that this is also the action that you use when assuming an effective golf stance! Allow the arms to relax and hang freely or allow them to rest next to the body as you bend forward. When you reach the lowest position, that is, where you feel the greatest stretch of the hamstrings on the posterior thighs, hold the position for two to three seconds. Then return to the upright position and relax.

Repeat the same movement and lower the trunk slightly more than previously if more flexibility is needed. For greater strengthening, hold light dumbbells in your hands to increase resistance.

To assist you in the early stages, have someone watch the position of your spine to be sure that you maintain the normal curvature in the lower spine as you bend over from the hips. If there is any rounding of the back, you should stop at that point and reassume the arched position. Remember, the slightly arched low back position is the normal, safe curvature position of the lumbar spine.

If you are accustomed to a rounded spine position, the normally curved spine position will feel uncomfortable. But after you practice it on a daily basis, it will become easier and more comfortable. Most importantly, you will then be able to hold a safe spine position during execution of the swing.

The good morning is especially important for women who are pregnant or who have a large bosom. The increased weight in front of the body makes it extremely important to have strong lower back and hip extensor muscles to hold not only the trunk erect but to hold the basic stance. By strengthening the lower back muscles, the normal position of the spine can be held comfortably for longer periods of time, which allows you to play a good game of golf without undue fatigue or danger of injury.

These exercises are some of the main exercises used to strengthen the muscles involved in maintaining a proper stance. However, there are still other exercises that can be done to strengthen the hip and lower back muscles. These exercises include the back raise, reverse back raise (in Chapter 10), and back raise with a twist (in Chapter 5).

CHAPTER
5

The Backswing

Role of the Backswing

An effective backswing plays an important role in delivering explosive power in the downswing. It is necessary preparation for a release of built-up energy. In exercise physiology, it is well understood that when a muscle is actively stretched, it will in turn contract with greater force. In golf, the muscles involved in the downswing are placed in a stretched position during the backswing. As a result of this active stretch, these muscles accumulate elastic energy, which is given back when the muscles contract in the downswing. To achieve your swing potential, you must take advantage of this phase of the swing. You must learn to utilize the effects of this active stretch and muscular contraction to generate more power with less energy expenditure.

When the club is brought up and back during the backswing, it creates a long pathway over which you can produce maximum clubhead speed. The exact length of the pathway depends on your midsection and shoulder flexibility, as well as muscle strength. It is also determined by the club you choose and the distance the shot demands. The muscles used to rotate the shoulders and hips to the rear, to bring the arms up and back, and to cock the wrists are for the most part found on the opposite side of the joints that are involved in the downswing.

Developing Your Explosive Potential

By increasing your flexibility and strengthening the muscles involved in the backswing, you will have a greatly enhanced ability to get a full wind-up (coiling) of the trunk and full-range arm and shoulder movement. The greater the trunk rotation and arm movement, the greater the distance over which you can generate the power needed in the downswing.

Exercises

The following strength and flexibility exercises focus specifically on the key actions involved in the backswing. These exercises can help you to enhance the power potential of your swing. (*Note:* All exercise movements throughout this book are based upon a right-handed player.)

- Shoulder twist
- Back raise with a twist
- Radial wrist flexion
- Shoulder joint active stretch: left shoulder
- Static hip adduction: right leg

The shoulder twist and back raise with a twist exercises primarily strengthen the lower back and serve to increase the degree of shoulder rotation as well as improve midsection flexibility. They are important for developing a tightly coiled upper trunk in preparation for the downswing.

The radial wrist flexion exercise, which duplicates the wrist cock, plays an important role in enabling you to bring the clubhead back farther while also holding the wrists in the cocked position longer. This helps prevent casting (early wrist break).

The shoulder joint active stretch exercise enables you to raise the left arm higher to achieve a longer backswing and still maintain a more compact body position. It represents an across-the-body shoulder stretch.

The static hip adduction exercise strengthens the muscles of the inner right leg. This is important for stabilizing the body and creating a firm right-side axis around which hip and shoulder rotation can take place for the coiling action.

Joint Action: Shoulder Rotation

Shoulder or trunk rotation to the rear is perhaps one of the most important actions in the backswing. This movement involves the low back muscles—more specifically, the erector spinae muscles on the right side of the lumbar spine. The strength of these muscles determines the amount of shoulder rotation that you can attain when you have adequate midsection flexibility. If these muscles are weak or if there is inadequate midsection flexibility, you will not be able to rotate the shoulders sufficiently to ensure a powerful downswing.

The shoulders should be in a side-facing position to the target; in other words, they should be in line with the target (see fig. 5.1a). At the top of the backswing, the shoulders should rotate approximately 90 degrees so that the back faces the target (see figs. 5.1b–c).

(a)

Figure 5.1   Shoulders in line with the target

(b)

Shoulders rotate 90 degrees at the top of the backswing.

(c)

Another view of 90-degree shoulder rotation

Notice that in figure 5.1b the golfer has slightly greater rotation of the shoulders and hips than the golfer in figure 5.1c. However, the golfer in figure b has less separation between the hip and shoulder than the golfer in figure c. Thus the golfer in figure c has more potential for the development of power.

(a)

Figure 5.2 Shoulder twist starting position

Shoulder Twist

For those with weak back musculature or limited midsection flexibility, one of the simplest exercises to strengthen the lower back muscles and develop some midsection flexibility is the shoulder twist with a pole or bar across the shoulders. To execute, assume a standing position with your feet slightly wider than shoulder-width apart. Hold a bar across the shoulders on outstretched arms. Bend over from the hips while maintaining the normal spinal curvature so that you have the same trunk angle as in the regular golf swing (see fig. 5.2a).

When in position, rotate to the right as far as possible, just as you do in the backswing (see fig. 5.2b). Be sure to keep the lumbar spine in its normal curvature (slightly arched) during execution. After reaching the farthest position, rotate as in the usual swing and then go as far as possible to the left (see fig. 5.2c). Go through a full range of motion.

Using a long pole across the shoulders on outstretched arms is most effective for ensuring a full range of motion. If you use a golf club on the shoulders or behind the back in the crooks of both elbows, it is difficult to get a full range of motion.

(b)

Rotate right.

(c)

Rotate left.

Caution: Rotating the shoulders with a rounded back (flexed spine) can be injurious to the lower back.

Back Raise with a Twist

A more advanced exercise than the shoulder twist with a pole is the back raise with a twist. In this exercise you rotate the shoulders directly against the pull of gravity, which creates greater resistance—and as a result, greater strength. It is an extremely effective exercise, a must for all golfers.

To execute, position yourself facedown on a Yessis Back Machine so that when your feet are secured, your pelvis will rest directly on top of the seat. This is needed to stabilize the pelvis so that the action is only in the waist when the shoulders are rotated. Your upper trunk should hang down at approximately a 60-degree angle with a long pole placed across the shoulders and held in place on outstretched arms (see fig. 5.3a). Your arms and trunk should form the letter *T*.

When you are ready, inhale and hold your breath as you raise the trunk slightly above the horizontal position. Hold this position and then rotate 90 degrees to the right (see fig. 5.3b). Twist back to the

(a)

Figure 5.3   Back raise with a twist starting position

(b)
Raise trunk then twist right.

(c)
Repeat to the left.

facedown position and then lower yourself to the initial position, exhaling as you do so.

After a momentary pause, inhale again and raise your trunk. When your body is horizontal, rotate up to 90 degrees to the opposite side (see fig. 5.3c). This is needed to help balance excessive muscular development on the right side of the lower back, a consequence of playing much golf. Turn back to the facedown position, lower your body, relax, and then repeat, twisting to alternate sides.

If a Yessis Back Machine is not available, you can use a high, sturdy table. When using a table, position yourself facedown so that the navel is at the far edge of the table, and have an assistant hold your legs down. Place a folded towel under your hips (lower abdomen) for a stronger effect. Execute in the same manner.

When you are sufficiently strong, you do not have to lower your trunk and then raise it before each twist. In this case, hold your body in the up position with the normal spinal curvature and then rotate the shoulders left and right a full 90 degrees. If additional development is needed on the right side, then limit your rotations to only this side. But be sure to do some rotations on the opposite side to balance your low back muscle development. A major muscular imbalance between your right and left sides can set you up for low back injury.

Note: Since the back raise exercise is one of the most important exercises for strengthening the lower back, I recommend that you also do this exercise, especially if you have a weak back. You should understand that the back raise is the only exercise in which you strengthen the lower back muscles through the full range of motion. The muscles on both sides of the spine are strengthened equally, which helps to prevent muscular imbalances. It is described in detail in Chapter 10.

For most golfers, the back raise is the best exercise not only for maintaining a strong lower back, but for rehabilitation and prevention of a low back injury. In fact, I have found that the back raise is perhaps the favorite back exercise of the thousands of golfers and athletes with whom I have worked.

Joint Action: Radial Wrist Flexion (Cocking the Wrists)

The wrist cock, also known as radial flexion, is needed to increase the rearward distance that the clubhead can travel in the backswing. The forearm muscles involved in this action are the flexor carpi radialis and the extensor carpi radialis. The wrist cock also places on stretch the ulna flexor muscles that will be used in the wrist break on the downswing (see figs. 5.4a–b).

(a)

Figure 5.4 Radial flexion increases the distance the clubhead can travel in the backswing.

(b)

The thumb sides of the wrists are closer toward the forearms. The club shaft forms a 90-degree angle with the arm.

In this action, the thumb sides of the wrists have moved closer toward the forearms, and the club shaft forms a 90-degree angle with the arm (see fig. 5.4b). In the address position, the club shaft and arms are almost in a straight line (see fig. 5.4a).

Radial Wrist Flexion

Stand with your arms alongside your body and hold a Strength Bar in one hand with the weighted end pointing to the front. Lower the weighted end as far as possible to the beginning position (see fig. 5.5a). Keep your arm straight and raise the weighted end of the bar as high as possible (see fig. 5.5b). Return to the initial position and repeat. Use only wrist action when doing this exercise. When done correctly, the range of motion is not great (less than 90 degrees).

Note: The length of the bar that is used plays an important role in regard to resistance and range of

motion. From practical experience, I have found that the 15-inch Strength Bar (depicted in the photographs) is best. When the bar is shorter (8 to 12 inches), you must use more resistance and the range of motion is less. If the bar is too long (20 or more inches), it becomes too difficult to handle with even the lightest weights. Keep in mind that the longer the bar, the greater the resistance at the end of the bar. To adjust the resistance, move your hand closer to the weights to make it easier, and move your hand farther away to make it harder to execute.

Joint Action: Horizontal Arm Adduction (Left Arm)

For maximum coiling and compactness in the backswing, the left arm should be fairly close to the chest at the end of the backswing. Bringing the left arm

(a)

Figure 5.5 Radial wrist flexion starting position

(b)

Keep your arms straight and raise the weighted end of the bar.

(a)

Figure 5.6 In address position, left arm is removed from chest.

(b)

The left arm moves closer to the chest at the top of the backswing.

across the body and in close is known as horizontal shoulder joint adduction. This action, in addition to allowing for a tight coiling action, also prepares the muscles to pull the left arm down and across explosively in the downswing. In the address position, you can see how far the left arm is removed from the chest (see fig. 5.6a). At the top of the backswing, the left arm appears close to the chest (see fig. 5.6b).

Shoulder Joint Active Stretch: Left Shoulder

To be able to bring the left arm in close to the chest to get a compact, coiled body, you should do the following active shoulder stretch with the Active Cords. Hold the handle attached to one end of the cord in the left hand and stand sideways to the attachment of the other end. Assume the golf stance and bring the left arm across the body. The attachment of the cord

at this time should be approximately shoulder-high and should have ample tension (see fig. 5.7a).

Hold the left arm in place and use the tension of the elastic cord to restrict any movement of the left arm. Then turn your body slowly into the left arm. Go as far as is comfortably possible and hold for two to four seconds (see fig. 5.7b). Then relax, back off, and repeat. Get a little tighter each time to bring the left arm in closer to the body.

Joint Action: Static Hip Adduction (Right Leg)

When taking the backswing, to prevent lateral weight shift to the rear and to ensure a tight coiling of the trunk around the right leg, it is important that the right leg remain stable. It must essentially be held in place throughout the backswing. The muscles involved here are the hip joint

(a)

Figure 5.7 Shoulder joint active stretch starting position

(b)

Turn your body slowly into the left arm.

adductors, and they must be strengthened in the isometric regimen so that they can maintain the static position (see figs. 5.8a–b).

Static Hip Adduction: Right Leg

In right leg adduction, you develop the isometric strength of the muscles needed to maintain a firm right leg, which will act as an axis of rotation for the hips and shoulders. At the same time, the firm right leg prevents the hips from shifting to the rear excessively.

To execute, attach the rubber cord to the ankle strap around the right leg and stand away from the attachment so that there is ample tension in the tubing. The tension should be sufficient to prevent you from easily moving the leg inward. Begin with your legs wider than in the initial stance (see fig. 5.9a).

When ready, inhale and hold your breath as you pull the right leg inward until the legs are stance-width (or closer) (see fig. 5.9b). Hold the inward pulling action of the right leg for four to six seconds. Then exhale and relax as you move the leg back to the

initial position to relieve some of the tension on the cord. Pause for several seconds and then repeat.

Joint Action: Arm Rotation

If you are capable of taking a full backswing, you already have the ability to rotate the arms as needed. I want to highlight the arm rotation so that you will better appreciate its significance in the downswing.

In the address position, the palms of the hands are facing one another and the thumbs are uppermost (see figs. 5.10a–b). As the hands approach hip height, the left arm rotates inward and the right arm rotates outward. These actions allow you to not only continue raising the arms in a side plane, but also to cock the wrists to provide for a longer clubhead pathway to the rear. At this time, no exercises are needed to enhance these actions. However, exercises to enhance arm rotation in the downswing are presented in Chapter 6.

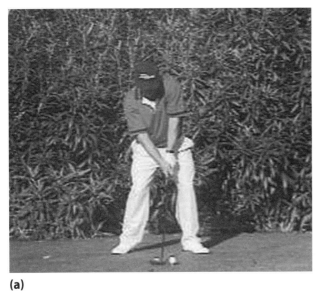

(a)

Figure 5.8   The right leg remains stable from address to backswing.

(b)

The right leg creates an axis of rotation for the hips and shoulders.

(a)

Figure 5.9   Static hip adduction starting position

(b)

Pull the right leg in to stance-width (or closer).

(a)

Figure 5.10   Arm rotation in the backswing

(b)

The left arm rotates inward and the right arm outward.

6

The Downswing

Role of the Downswing

Once you have executed a proper backswing, you have placed yourself in an effective position to begin the downswing. Remain mindful that the movements involved in the backswing play a critical role in preparing appropriate muscle groups for immediate action. Now, we turn our focus to the most important phase of the golf swing—the downswing.

The downswing marks the phase in which power and explosiveness are generated in the swing and transmitted into the ball. What takes place here will determine the outcome of your shot.

Developing an Explosive Downswing

It is important to have not only good technique, but sufficient force for each action to build an explosive downswing. When this force is added to the preceding amount of force generated, it culminates in maximum clubhead speed during contact. To generate the force needed in each joint action, you must increase the strength of the muscles involved. This applies to not only your weak actions, but also your strong ones. The increases in strength and, in some cases, flexibility in the joint actions must be integrated into the entire swing to make it explosive and controlled.

Exercises

The following specialized strength and flexibility exercises duplicate the major actions and movements that take place in the downswing.

- Hip joint abduction
- Hip rotation
- Reverse trunk twist
- Russian twist
- Left arm abduction
- Right arm adduction
- Wrist supination and pronation
- Ulnar flexion
- Lateral rotation: left arm
- Medial rotation: right arm
- Finger flexion
- Wrist flexion and extension

The hip slide is the action for weight shift that begins the buildup of force and establishes the new axis for forward hip rotation. The hip slide and hip rotation "clear the hips," which not only produces greater force but sets you up for even more forceful shoulder rotation. The greater the hip rotation before the shoulder rotation begins, the more force that can be generated! By strengthening the muscles that act on the hips, you will be able to produce even greater explosive force and simultaneously eliminate stress on the lower back and shoulders.

The hip slide and hip and shoulder rotation exercises are most important in producing explosive force. Other exercises in this chapter deal with arm and wrist actions, which are also needed to produce force (especially the wrist break). Their main role is to help you make good ball contact.

For example, the arm exercises (right arm adduction and left arm abduction) duplicate the arm action that follows shoulder rotation to bring the club into the hitting area. The medial (inward) and lateral (outward) rotation of the right and left arms, respectively, bring the clubhead around to the square position prior to contact, contribute additional force, and help to prevent injury to the shoulder. Hand supination and pronation (the wrist roll), especially right hand pronation, ensures that the clubhead returns to the square-to-the-target position.

The ulnar flexion exercise, which duplicates the wrist break, is extremely important in producing force prior to contact. Finger grip strength is needed to ensure that all the forces generated by the body are transferred to the clubhead and then to the ball. A strong grip also prevents turning of the clubface during ball contact, especially when there is off-center contact.

Joint Action: Hip Slide

The hip slide or weight shift (weight transfer) is the first action in the downswing. It is generally known as "getting your hips into the shot." The main action involved is right hip joint abduction, which involves the gluteus medius and minimus muscles located on the sides of the hips. In addition, these muscles are involved in holding your pelvis level during the swing and as you walk the course.

In the address position, the hips are between the feet. During the backswing, the hips remain in place or move back slightly to be closer to the right leg (see figs. 6.1–6.2). In the hip slide, the hips remain level

Figure 6.1 The hips move closer to the right leg.

Figure 6.2 The hips remain in place.

Figure 6.3 The hip slide

and move forward so that they are over or more on the front leg (see fig. 6.3). This indicates the weight shift. Note that immediately afterward (in some golfers, even simultaneously with this action), there is also hip rotation. As a result, there is a change in leg–hip position. In essence, the legs adjust to accommodate the new positioning of the hips but remain bent in the knees. The legs cannot initiate forward action of the body. In fact, early driving of the left knee forward will interfere with a timely hip slide.

Hip Joint Abduction

Secure one end of an elastic cord to the special hip belt placed around the hips. Stand sideways to the attachment of the other end of the cord fixed about hip-high and with ample tension. Assume the golf stance with your right hip facing the fixed attachment (see fig. 6.4a).

When you are ready, inhale, keep the spine angle, and push the hips forward over the left (front) leg (see fig. 6.4b). Keep the hips level during the push so that the action is isolated in the right hip joint. Your head and shoulders will also shift a little. Exhale as you

(a)
Figure 6.4 Hip joint abduction starting position

(b)
Push the hips forward over the left leg.

return to the initial position, relax, and then repeat. When doing this exercise, it is important that you keep your basic stance at all times, especially holding the shoulders in place. If the shoulders move backward, that is analogous to leaning backward as you execute the swing.

Joint Action: Forward Hip Rotation

As the weight shift slows down, the hips begin to rotate to the left; they accelerate forward toward the target. When most of the weight is on the left leg, this involves mainly the medial rotators of the left hip joint. The left leg becomes the axis of rotation for the hips to create the longest possible lever (from left to right hip) to produce the greatest force.

Since the pelvis rotated to the right in the backswing to place the left hip medial rotator muscles on stretch, you must rotate the hips back to the initial position and beyond. The muscles involved in this action (medial hip rotation) are the tensor fascia latae and the gluteus minimus. They are located on the outside of the left thigh and hip.

When the forward hip rotation takes place with the spine held in its normal curvature, there is no additional pressure on the spine. This also holds true when the following shoulder rotation occurs not only in the downswing but in the follow-through. In essence, the initial hip slide and hip rotation (clearing the hips) give you more effective alignment of the spine for the following actions, which in turn helps to prevent back problems.

If your weight shift is limited before rotating the hips forward, your weight will be balanced more on both legs. As a result, there will not only be medial rotation in the left hip joint, but there will also be lateral rotation in the right hip joint. This latter action involves the gluteus maximus and the outward rotators of the hip.

When both hip joints are in action, the spine is the axis of rotation rather than the left hip (leg) and left side of the body. As a result, less force is created because of the shortened lever arm of the pelvis and shoulders. In this case, as the hips rotate around the spine, the left hip moves backward and the right hip moves forward. The same thing happens with the shoulders.

It is most important to shift and have the hips rotate forward prior to the shoulder rotation. This is "clearing the hips." The more the hips can rotate forward while the shoulders stay back, the greater the upper-body torque and the greater the ensuing force from shoulder rotation. This separation of the shoulders and hips is commonly known as the X-factor.

During the backswing, it is possible that the hips may rotate back but not fully (see figs. 6.5–6.6). The hips should shift and rotate forward (see figs. 6.7–6.8). This indicates that medial rotation in the left hip joint has occurred, providing more power in the swing.

Hip Rotation

One of the simplest exercises for hip rotation is done with Active Cords. The hip rotation exercise is excellent for improving the ability of the hips to slide forward and rotate through early and quickly.

To do this exercise, attach the nonslip belt around the hips (about 2 inches above the pubic bone) and secure it firmly. Do not place the belt around the waist! Attach one end of the cord to the ring in front of the right hip, and stand with your right side to the door or support where the other end of the cord is attached at hip height (see fig. 6.9a).

When ready, rotate the hips slightly to the rear as in the backswing while still retaining tension on the tubing. Then shift your weight onto the left leg (slide the hips forward) to create more tension in the tubing. As you do this, turn the hips to the left against the resistance of the tubing (see fig. 6.9b). This is a great exercise for learning not only correct technique, but for getting more power in the hip turn.

Joint Action: Shoulder Rotation

In shoulder rotation, a very powerful action because of the mass being accelerated, the abdominal oblique muscles are strongly involved. More specifically, they are the right external oblique and the

Figure 6.5 The hips rotate back.

Figure 6.6 The hips may not rotate back fully.

Figure 6.7 The hips shift and rotate forward.

Figure 6.8 Medial rotation in the left hip joint

(a)

Figure 6.9 Hip rotation starting position

(b)

Turn the hips left against the resistance of the tubing.

left internal oblique. Recall that these muscles are placed on stretch during the backswing and become even more tensed as the hips rotate forward while the shoulders stay back. This separation is needed to generate more explosive shoulder rotational force in the downswing.

In the backswing, the shoulders should rotate about 90 degrees to the rear (see fig. 6.10a). In the downswing, the shoulders rotate forward, toward the target, while the arms are held back (see fig. 6.10b). Note that the arms move forward simultaneously with the shoulder rotation. Keep in mind that the arms and shoulders were brought back full range in the backswing. Thus, when the shoulders go into action, the arms must also go into motion. This action places the arms in motion, but it is not an arm action (this occurs later).

When shoulder rotation occurs simultaneously with hip rotation, less force is generated. This is one of the main reasons why it is important that the hips be cleared and rotated before the shoulder rotation begins. If you shift and rotate the hips first, the following actions will have more speed, and as a result, will greatly increase the distance you can hit the ball.

Reverse Trunk Twist

For most golfers, the best exercise to strengthen the abdominal oblique muscles and to simultaneously improve midsection flexibility is the reverse trunk twist. This exercise can improve your swing more than most other exercises, and, as a bonus, will give you a more narrow waist and a flatter abdominal wall!

(a)

Figure 6.10   The shoulders rotate 90 degrees to the rear in the backswing.

(b)

The shoulders rotate forward while the arms are held back.

Lie faceup on the floor with your arms out to the sides and your palms down. Your arms should be perpendicular to your trunk so that your body forms the letter *T*. Raise your legs so that your thighs are vertical and together. Bend the knees slightly to accommodate tight hamstrings and to make execution easier. Maintain this leg–trunk position throughout the entire exercise (see fig. 6.11a).

When you are ready, lower your legs to one side while continuing to hold the 90-degree angle in your hip joints. Touch the floor with the outside of the foot (or knee, if the knees are bent), keeping your shoulders and arms in full contact with the floor (see fig. 6.11b). Then raise the legs up and over to the other side and repeat in an alternating manner (see fig. 6.11c). Exhale as you lower the legs, and inhale and hold your breath as you raise the legs.

Only half of this exercise duplicates the muscle action in the downswing. However, you should do the exercise on both sides to maintain body and muscle symmetry and to have a supple and well-aligned spine. If the almost straight leg position makes the exercise too difficult, bend the knees more. However, be sure to keep the thighs vertical at all times. If your shoulders rise up as you do the exercise, have someone hold them down (see figs. 6.11d–f).

When you work out with Active Cords, you can also do a supplementary strength exercise for the obliques. Hold one end of the cord in your right hand with the elbow bent 90 degrees in line with the shoulders and with the shoulders rotated 90 degrees to the rear. Lock the hips in place and rotate the shoulders to the contact position.

Russian Twist

The Russian twist is for those who have adequate strength of the lower back and abdominal muscles. To do this exercise without assistance, you should use a Yessis Back Machine. This is the only machine that has the adjustability needed to fit all body types and sizes.

Adjust the unit so that when you sit with your pelvis directly on top of the rounded seat, your legs will be straight when your feet are placed between the rollers. Lower your trunk backward to the horizontal position so that your entire body is straight

(a)

Figure 6.11 Reverse trunk twist—maintain trunk–leg position throughout the exercise.

(b)

Keep shoulders and arms in full contact with the floor.

(c)

Alternate sides, touching the floor with the outside of the foot.

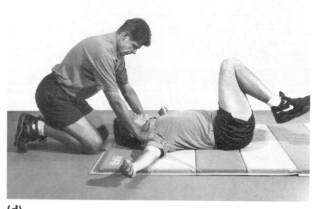

(d)

Bend the knees to make execution easier.

(e)

A partner keeps shoulders and arms from lifting.

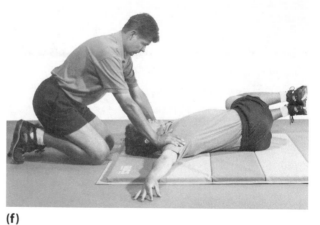

(f)

The outside of the knees touch the floor.

and basically parallel to the floor. Raise your arms so that they are perpendicular to your trunk (see fig. 6.12a).

Rotate the shoulders to the right a full 90 degrees and then back, continuing the movement up and over to the other side until your arms are once again parallel to the floor (see figs. 6.12b–c). Alternate the right and left shoulder rotation movements until you have completed the desired number of repetitions. Hold a light weight in your hands for greater resistance. (For most golfers, extra resistance is not needed.) When you rotate upward from the right side, you duplicate the muscular action in the downswing. However, both sides should be exercised for muscle symmetry and maintaining correct spinal alignment.

The Russian twist is considered a highly specialized golf exercise as it duplicates a major swing action (shoulder rotation), having the same type of muscular contraction and range of motion. It can dramatically increase the distance you can hit the ball.

In this exercise, you must hold your body in proper alignment at all times. If you find yourself weakening and your back hyperextending, then immediately stop doing the exercise. In this, as in other rotational exercises, when you rotate with your spine in a flexed or hyperextended position, there are great shearing and compression forces that may injure the spinal discs or vertebrae. Always maintain the natural spinal curvature.

....

Joint Action: Left Arm Abduction and Right Arm Adduction

The shoulder rotation initiates the arm and club movement in the early phase of the downswing. As the arms reach about chest level, they begin their own action, which continues through the contact zone. The left arm undergoes abduction, which involves mainly the left posterior deltoid and long head of the triceps, together with the teres minor and infraspinatus muscles of the rotator cuff. The right arm undergoes adduction, which involves the right latissimus dorsi, teres major, and lower pectoralis major.

Since both hands grip the club, one arm cannot act without the other. Thus, when the arms are in

(a)

Figure 6.12 Russian twist starting position

(b)

Rotate the shoulders to the right a full 90 degrees.

(c)

Continue the movement up and over to the left.

action, both the left and the right participate to maintain the shoulder–arms triangle. In the downswing, the left arm is fairly close to the chest and the right arm is bent with the elbow slightly away from the body (see figs. 6.13–6.14). It is then possible that the arms move across the body (see fig. 6.15). In addition, the right arm is extended and closer to the body. Both arms are now fairly straight in preparation for their next action, rotation.

Figure 6.13   In the downswing, the left arm is close to the chest.

Left Arm Abduction

A basic exercise with the elastic cord duplicates the left arm abduction movement. Use of the cord allows you to move the arm in the same manner as in the swing. To execute, secure one end of the rubber cord approximately hip-high or slightly higher. Stand in a side-facing position holding the cord with your left arm across the body. Hold the handle with the palm facing to the rear. Keep the left arm straight and hold the handle (grip) on the right side of the body (see fig. 6.16a).

Be sure that you have sufficient tension in the tubing to create the necessary resistance. When ready, inhale slightly more than usual, hold the body stable, and then pull the left arm down and then up as it moves across the body. This simulates the arm's movement during the golf swing (see fig. 6.16b). Be sure to remain bent over from the hips as in the golf stance so that the exercise duplicates what happens in the actual swing. You can also shift weight and rotate the hips before executing the left arm pull.

Right Arm Adduction

The right arm straightens and undergoes adduction as it moves down and across the body. One of the best exercises to duplicate this action is right arm adduction with rubber tubing. It allows you to follow the same pathway as in the full swing.

Figure 6.14   The right arm is bent.

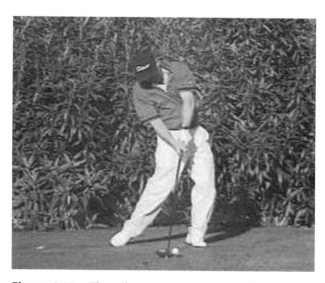

Figure 6.15   Then the arms move across the body.

(a)

Figure 6.16 Left arm abduction starting position

(b)

Pull the arm down and across the body.

To execute, stand sideways to the fixed attachment, which is approximately hip-high. Grasp the handle and stand far enough from the attachment so that there is tension in the tubing when in the ready position (see fig. 6.17a). Inhale slightly more than usual, and, while keeping your right arm straight, pull the handle down and across the body (see fig. 6.17b). Exhale and relax as you move the arm back to the initial position, under control. Repeat for the necessary repetitions.

Joint Action: Wrist Roll

As the arms move into the hitting area, they are held basically straight (after the right arm straightens). Because of this, the turning of the hands is a consequence of the arm rotation that takes place in the shoulder joints (lateral rotation of the left arm and medial rotation of the right arm). However, some golfers maintain slightly bent arms prior to and during contact. In this case, there is strong pronation

of the right hand and supination of the left. In supination, you turn the hand palm-up; in pronation, you turn the hand palm-down. Both supination and pronation occur together with the same arm rotation.

Note that in the backswing, the right arm underwent elbow flexion with hand supination in order to bring the clubhead back to its farthest position. Thus in the downswing, not only does the right arm straighten, but the right hand undergoes pronation as the arm extends and moves into the hitting area.

Notice the positions of the right and left forearms in the following figures. In figure 6.18, the right palm and the back of the left hand are visible. In figure 6.19, the right and left thumbs are visible. This indicates that the left forearm supinated (palm turned up) and the right forearm pronated (palm turned down). Also, the elbows remained slightly bent throughout this action.

To determine if you are mainly a supinator and pronator of the forearms (hands) or if you use strong medial and lateral rotation of the arms, check the

(a)

Figure 6.17 Right arm adduction starting position

(b)

Keep the right arm straight and pull down and across the body.

Figure 6.18 The right palm and the back of the left hand are visible.

Figure 6.19 The right and left thumbs are visible.

(a)

Figure 6.20 Wrist supination and pronation starting position

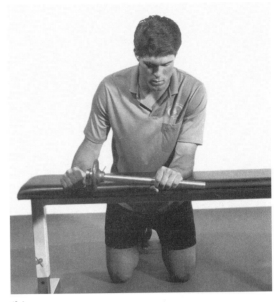

(b)

Turn your hand palm-down (pronation).

arm position immediately prior to and during the hit. If the elbows are bent at impact, mainly supination and pronation occurs. If the arms are straight, mainly medial and lateral rotation of the arms takes place. In most cases there is a little of both.

Wrist Supination and Pronation

Execution of supination and pronation can be done separately or at the same time. For convenience, they will be described here as one exercise. Kneel in front of the long side of an exercise bench. Place the forearm to be exercised across the bench so that your wrist and hand are clear of the bench surface. Hold a Strength Bar in your hand in a neutral grip—that is, with your thumb uppermost, and the bar vertical with the weight at the top end. This is the starting position (fig. 6.20a).

When ready, turn your hand palm-down (pronation) until the shaft of the bar is level with the bench, or slightly below it if you have good flexibility (see fig. 6.20b). Maintain the forearm and elbow in contact with the bench and then rotate the forearm and hand in the opposite direction (supination). The palm should now be turned up, so that once again the shaft of the Strength Bar is level with the bench or slightly

(c)

Turn your hand palm-up (supination).

below it (see fig. 6.20c). Repeat, alternating left and right sides for the necessary number of repetitions. Keep your shoulders over the elbow so that you maintain a 90-degree angle in the arm and keep the forearm in contact with the bench. Do the exercise with both left and right arms.

Figure 6.21   The wrists are cocked in the initial phase of the downswing.

Figure 6.22   The wrist break begins when the hands are hip height.

When using the Strength Bar, you can change the resistance by moving the hand closer for less resistance and farther away from the weighted end for greater resistance. Also, supination and pronation is a valuable exercise for preventing and treating wrist and elbow problems, especially golfers (tennis) elbow. Thus, even if you do not emphasize this action in your swing, you should do supination and pronation for the prevention of injury.

Joint Action: Wrist Break (Uncocking the Wrists)

The wrists, which were cocked (radially flexed to produce a 90-degree angle between the arms and clubshaft) on the backswing, remain in this position in the initial phases of the downswing (see fig. 6.21). The wrist break, which should be forceful if it is to contribute power and accuracy, begins when the hands are approximately hip height (see figure 6.22) and ends just prior to contact (see fig. 6.23). In this action, the pinkie sides of the hands move toward

the forearms. The clubshaft and arms nearly appear as a straight line (see fig. 6.23). The wrist break is known as ulnar flexion, which involves the flexor carpi ulnaris and the extensor carpi ulnaris muscles.

Ulnar Flexion

To execute ulnar flexion, which duplicates the wrist break action, stand with your feet approximately shoulder-width apart and hold a Strength Bar in one hand alongside the body. The weighted end of the bar should point to the rear and be lowered so that your hand is cocked, in maximal radial flexion (see fig. 6.24a).

Keep your arm straight and raise the weighted end of the Strength Bar as high as possible (see fig. 6.24b). At this time you should also feel the triceps undergo contraction. Relax the muscles slightly and return to the original position, keeping the weight under control at all times. Pause and then repeat for the necessary repetitions. Do the exercise with both arms since both wrists are involved in this action.

Figure 6.23 The wrist break ends just prior to contact.

Joint Action: Arm Rotation

As you bring the club back in the backswing, the left arm is turned inward and the right arm outward to raise the arms sufficiently high and to cock the wrists. These actions also place the opposing muscles on stretch to more forcefully rotate the arms back to the initial position.

Thus, in the downswing the left arm turns outward (lateral rotation) and the right arm turns inward (medial rotation) to bring the clubhead back to the square-to-the-ball position.

It is possible to see the back of the left arm (back of palm and elbow) and the front of the right arm (palm side of forearm and upper arm) in figure 6.25. The arms then rotate (left arm outward, right arm inward) until just before and during impact so that the thumb and thumb side of the left arm is visible,

(a)

Figure 6.24 Ulnar flexion starting position

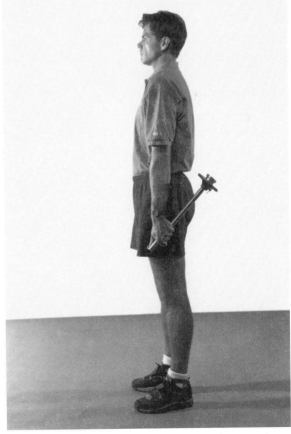

(b)

Keep your arm straight and raise the weighted end of the bar.

as is the right thumb and thumb side of the forearm and arm (see fig. 6.26). Note that some of the turn may also be due to supination and pronation. In essence, the left arm is straight and rotated outward, so that the back of the hand travels toward the target. The right arm is straight and rotated inward so that the palm side of the hand travels toward the target.

Note that if you do not fully rotate the left and right arms, the clubhead remains open and may cause a slice. Too much arm rotation can close the clubface, causing a hook.

Lateral Rotation: Left Arm

To execute left arm lateral rotation, assume your golf stance with the left arm raised forward. When in position, hold the Strength Bar with the weighted end uppermost and with the hand holding the non-weighted end (see fig. 6.27a). Rotate the left arm inward so that the weighted end is lowered toward the midline of the body. This is the starting position (see fig. 6.27b). From this position, rotate the bar back up to the vertical position to duplicate the action of the left arm in the downswing. Then repeat. To max-

imize development of the rotator cuff muscles, go through a full range of motion (see fig. 6.27c).

Medial Rotation: Right Arm

To execute right arm medial rotation, hold the bar in the same manner as for the lateral rotation exercise, but in the right hand. Execute in the same manner, emphasizing the raising of the weight from the outside so that your right arm is laterally rotated, then rotating the arm to the vertical or medial rotation.

These exercises are excellent for preventing rotator cuff muscle injuries. In these exercises, which duplicate what occurs in the golf swing, you strengthen the muscles as they are used. The effect on your swing will be immediate!

Note that the left arm undergoes medial rotation in the backswing and lateral rotation in the downswing and follow-through. The right arm undergoes lateral rotation in the backswing and then medial rotation in the downswing, which then continues into the follow-through. Because of this, you can do the exercise going through a full range of motion to work the muscles as needed in all three phases of the

Figure 6.25 The back of the left arm and the front of the right arm are visible.

Figure 6.26 The left arm rotates outward, the right inward.

(a)

Figure 6.27   Lateral rotation starting position

(b)

Assume the golf stance and hold the nonweighted end of the bar.

(c)

Maximize development of the rotator cuff muscles by going through the full range of motion.

swing. For example, rotate the arm through the full range in both medial and lateral rotation. Do the exercise with both the left and right arm.

Joint Action: Finger Grip

An aspect of the swing that is usually overlooked is the hand (finger) grip before contact. Close examination of the grip shows that it is mainly the index and middle fingers of the right hand and the pinkie, ring, and middle fingers of the left hand that make full contact on the club. The initial grip is relaxed so that you have a good feel for the club and club position. However, during ball contact you must have a strong (if not tight) grip and firm wrists to ensure that all the forces developed in the downswing are transferred to the ball.

A loose or relaxed grip at contact will dissipate the accumulated force, and as a result will decrease your hitting power. Strengthening the fingers that make contact with the club can, however, help give you a better feel for the club as well as a more secure grip. Most important, you will be able to get greater distance and accuracy in your hits, and the chances of the clubhead turning during contact, especially off-center contact, will be diminished greatly.

Finger Flexion

To exercise the fingers, use Exer Rings so that the fingers can be strengthened in several ways with the various rings available. For example, place a round ring against the middle pads of the fingers to be exercised (or all of the fingers) and the base of the thumb and palm (see fig. 6.28a). When in position, squeeze the resilient ring until your hand is in a fist or the isolated fingers are fully curled. The ring at this time should resemble the shape of a paper clip (see fig. 6.28b). Then relax your grip, and as the ring resumes its round shape, repeat. Squeeze and relax in a steady rhythm.

To strengthen the index and middle fingers, hold the ring between the tips of the fingers and thumb and squeeze the ring flat and then relax and repeat as needed (see figs. 6.29a–b). To strengthen the ring and pinkie fingers, hold the lighter flat ring between

(a)

Figure 6.28   Finger flexion

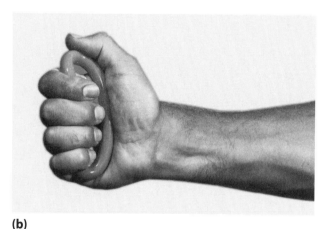

(b)

Squeeze the ring until your hand forms a fist.

(a)

Figure 6.29   Index and middle fingers

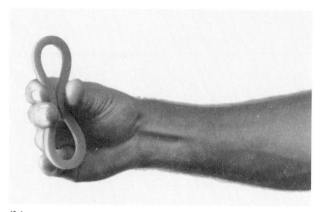

(b)

Squeeze the ring flat.

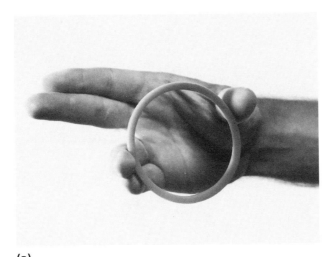

(a)

Figure 6.30   Ring and pinkie fingers

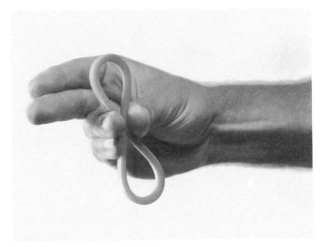

(b)

Squeeze the ring so that it forms a figure-eight.

these fingers and the thumb (see fig. 6.30a). Squeeze the ring so that it forms a figure-eight (see fig. 6.30b) and then relax the fingers and return to the original position.

To strengthen the thumb in a pressing action, hold a flat ring on the tips of all the fingers. Place the fingers on a table or your thigh and then press down with the thumb (see figs. 6.31a–b).

With Exer Rings, you can work any finger in any of its actions. Also, the rings can be used in warm water when your muscles are warm and pliable. Because of

this, they have great value in rehabilitation, and especially for players with arthritis.

Joint Action: Wrist Flexion and Extension

In addition to strong fingers, the flexor and extensor muscles of the wrist must be strong in order to hold the hands in position as contact occurs. At this time,

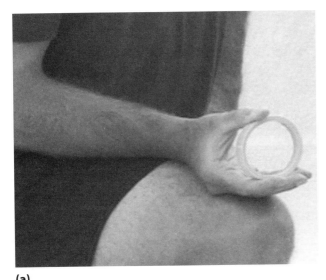

(a)

Figure 6.31   The thumb

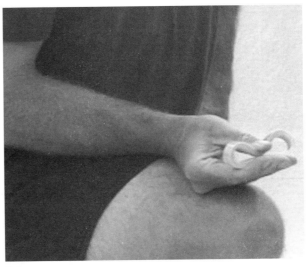

(b)

Place the fingers on your thigh and press down with the thumb.

Figure 6.32 Wrist flexion—compress the rings.

Figure 6.33 Wrist extension—pull the rings apart.

the muscular contractions are static. Thus, to duplicate the hand position, it is necessary to do isometric contractions of the wrist flexors and extensors.

Wrist Flexion and Extension

To work the wrist flexor muscles, hold two Exer Rings in the hands with the forearms in basically a vertical position with the elbows pointing down. There should be a great deal of tension in the rings so that you will have to squeeze very hard in an attempt to compress the rings. Hold for four to six seconds, relax, and then repeat (see fig. 6.32).

To work the wrist extensor muscles, hold the Exer Rings in the same position as just described. Instead of squeezing the rings together, however, make an attempt to pull them apart. Hold for four to six seconds, relax, and then repeat (see fig. 6.33).

CHAPTER 7

The Follow-Through

Role of the Follow-Through

The follow-through ensures maximum speed of the clubhead through the contact area to produce an explosive hit. If you did not follow through during the swing, you would have to slow down the club prior to ball contact so that it would stop immediately after contact is made with the ball. This would produce much less force and, consequently, much less distance. In addition, any sudden attempt to stop the club after its momentum has reached maximum force (speed) can result in injury.

A full follow-through keeps the clubhead in contact with the golf ball as long as possible so that greater force can be applied to the ball. Any slowing down of the clubhead during contact decreases the distance you can hit the ball. The follow-through also ensures a fluid pathway through the hitting area. Any effort to modify the follow-through will result in diminished accuracy and ultimately hurt your golf swing.

Developing an Explosive Follow-Through

In general, the greater the clubhead speed, the greater the follow-through. However, this is also dependent upon the strength of your muscles since they play a major role in not only increasing but in decreasing clubhead speed.

When the ball is contacted, your body is basically stationary with only the arms and wrists in action. After contact, the arms continue their forward and upward movement following the club. After the arms, the shoulders continue to rotate forward followed by the hips, and finally the rear foot leaves the ground as your weight ends up on the forward leg.

Momentum is responsible for the movement in the follow-through, and no muscles are actively involved to produce the range of motion. Specific muscles are, however, stretched in an effort to slow down the club. As the muscles stretch, they contract eccentrically, developing tension as they lengthen.

This muscle tension, which increases with the range of motion, is responsible for slowing down and stopping the club in a safe manner. In essence, the muscles continue to contract eccentrically with greater and greater force and eventually become strong enough to stop the arms, body, and club. The rate of stretch is quite high, and if you do not have sufficient eccentric strength, the force of the momentum (especially in a big swing) can easily cause an injury to the muscles or joints.

The amount of muscle and connective tissue stretching depends upon the strength of the muscles and how much active stretch they can undergo in the follow-through. For example, if you are an arm swinger, most of the stretch will be in the back of the shoulder muscles. If you use hip and trunk rotation to a greater extent, then you will also stretch in the abdominal and lower back muscles to slow down and stop the body movements. The muscles involved in these movements are usually antagonistic to the muscles used in the downswing. As a result, for every major joint action in the downswing, the muscles that perform the opposite action undergo a strong muscle tension stretch to stop the movement in the follow-through.

Since the main function of the follow-through is to dissipate the forces generated in the downswing, any development of additional strength is used to slow down the club and body movements in order to finish in a balanced, nonstressful position. Thus the purpose of the specialized exercises that duplicate the follow-through actions is to ensure a full follow-through and to prevent injury. The full range of motion for maximum dissipation of the accumulated forces is needed.

Exercises

The following specialized strength and flexibility exercises duplicate the major actions and movements that take place in the follow-through.

- Standing row
- Reverse fly
- Side bend without hip slide; side bend with hip slide

- Yessis Back Machine sit-ups
- Large ball sit-ups
- Backward overhead medicine ball toss

The key exercises to fulfill these goals in the follow-through are the reverse fly, the side bend, and the Yessis Back Machine sit-ups. The reverse fly (along with the medial and lateral arm rotation as described for the downswing in Chapter 6) is especially important in prevention of rotator cuff injuries. The muscles involved in the exercise (teres minor and infraspinatus) must be strengthened to withstand the violent stretch that occurs in the back of the right shoulder during the follow-through.

The side bend is important for prevention of back injuries and to allow for complete weight shift, especially if you use the hips to maximize explosive force. The Yessis Back Machine sit-ups are needed to strengthen the abdominals as they are used to limit the ending position of the follow-through (the reverse-C posture).

Joint Action: Right Arm Horizontal Adduction

In the downswing, the right arm moves down and across the body (adduction) and then moves up and across in the follow-through. The right arm crosses the body with the thumb more or less pointed directly forward (see fig. 7.1a). The right arm is in front of the left shoulder, and the hand is turned inward—you can now see the back and the pinkie side of the hand (see fig. 7.1b). To slow down and to stop the right arm, the infraspinatus, teres minor, and posterior deltoid muscles are involved.

The infraspinatus and teres minor muscles, located on the back of the right shoulder and arm, also play very important roles in other phases of the swing. In the backswing, they rotate the right arm outward and bring the right arm to the rear of the body. If these muscles are tight in the left shoulder, they will limit how closely you can bring the left arm to the body, which is important for a compact coiling action in the backswing. Note that the infraspinatus and teres minor muscles of the left shoulder are also involved in rotating the left arm outward in the downswing (which brings the club into the

(a)

Figure 7.1 The right arm crosses the body with the thumb pointed forward.

(b)

The right arm is in front of the left shoulder.

square-to-the-ball position). They have many roles. Because of the bending of the left arm in the follow-through, the forces acting on the left shoulder are minimal and are not discussed here.

The right infraspinatus and teres minor muscles are often injured in the follow-through because they undergo a very powerful eccentric stretch to slow down the right arm and the golf club. Because these muscles are relatively small and usually underdeveloped, they are most often the ones that become injured. The other muscles that contract eccentrically to assist in stopping the arm include the latissimus dorsi, middle and posterior deltoid, and teres major. These muscles are fairly large and usually much stronger than the smaller rotator cuff muscles.

Standing Row

One of the best exercises to strengthen the infraspinatus, teres minor, and posterior deltoid muscles as they are used in the follow-through is the standing row. To execute, assume a standing position facing the attachment of an Active Cord and holding the handle in the right hand. The arms should be fully

extended with tension on the tubing when you are ready to begin (see fig. 7.2a).

Inhale and hold your breath to stabilize the body, and then pull the handle (tubing) toward you and back by bending the elbow. Concentrate on pulling the elbow beyond the back to fully contract and shorten the muscles (see fig. 7.2b). Keep the arm in line with the shoulders as you pull backward. After reaching the rearmost position, exhale and slowly return to the initial position under control. Repeat as needed.

Reverse Fly

If working with dumbbells, you can do the reverse fly. To execute, assume a facedown position on a high bench with the arms hanging straight down. Hold light dumbbells in your hands (see fig. 7.3a). When you are ready, inhale and hold your breath as you keep the arms straight, and raise them sideways until they are above the level of the back (see fig. 7.3b). After reaching the highest position, exhale and slowly lower the arms back to the initial position.

(a)

Figure 7.2 Standing row starting position

(b)

Pull the elbow beyond the back.

Joint Action: Lateral Spinal Flexion (Side Bending)

If you have a powerful weight shift and hip turn, your spine undergoes side bending in the follow-through (as well as in the downswing). As a result, after the shoulders rotate forward, there is usually hyperextension of the spine. This action is not dangerous if within your normal range of motion and if the hips are cleared prior to the shoulder rotation.

However, if the range of motion exceeds your capabilities or if the sequence of actions is interrupted, a back injury may occur. Thus it is important to strengthen the muscles that are involved in these actions so that if you do experience any unexpected forces, the muscles will be able to handle them safely.

The key muscle involved in side bending is the quadratus lumborum. It is very important to golfers since it provides lateral stability to the spine and is many times a culprit in low back problems. By strengthening this muscle together with the side abdominal (oblique) and low back (erector spinae) muscles, you not only enhance the side bending

after the weight shift, but also help prevent injury to the lower back.

At the start of the downswing, the hips are in line with the shoulders (see fig. 7.4a). You can see a side curve of the body with the hips in front after the hip slide (see fig. 7.4b). The sideward-facing reverse-*C* curve changes as you go into the follow-through (see fig. 7.4c) and finally becomes a forward-facing reverse-*C* curve (see fig. 7.4d).

Side Bend Without Hip Slide

One of the simplest exercises to strengthen the quadratus lumborum and the other muscles involved in the sideward-facing reverse-*C* curve is the side bend with a dumbbell in one hand or with Active Cords. The free arm should be left alongside the body or placed behind the head with your body weight balanced on both feet and your pelvic girdle firmly in place at all times.

When using elastic cords to execute side bends, stand with one end of the cord under your feet so that it is firmly secured. Hold the other end in your

(a)

Figure 7.3   Reverse fly starting position

(b)

Keep the arms straight and raise them sideways above the back.

(a)

Figure 7.4   The start of the downswing

(b)

After the hip slide

(c)

Into the follow-through

(d)

Forward-facing reverse-C curve

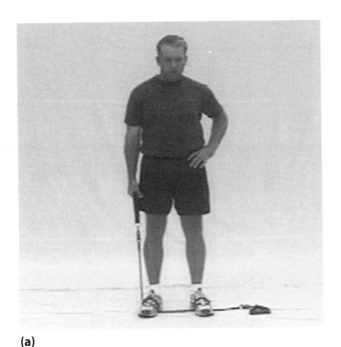

(a)

Figure 7.5 Side bend without hip slide starting position

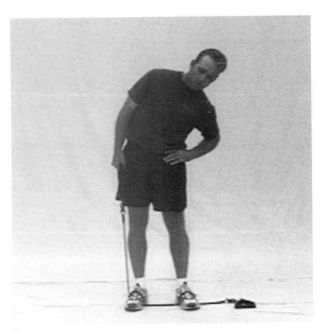

(b)

Bend away from the cord keeping hips in place.

(c)

Bend over the side with the elastic cord.

hand on the same side of the body and adjust the length so that there is tension (see fig. 7.5a). When ready, inhale and bend to the opposite side as far as possible while keeping the hips in place (see fig. 7.5b). Return to the original position, and without stopping

exhale as you bend over on the side of the elastic cord and repeat (see fig. 7.5c).

Side Bend with Hip Slide

A more advanced version of the side bend exercise is to slide the hips laterally as you bend sideways. Assume a well-balanced standing position while holding a dumbbell in one hand (see fig. 7.6a). Lower your shoulders (upper trunk) and shift hips as far as possible away from the arm holding the dumbbell (see fig. 7.6b). When you reach the bottom position, inhale and raise your trunk up and over toward the other side as far as possible (see fig. 7.6c). Exhale as you lower the shoulders and shift the hips and then quickly inhale as you begin to rise up and shift to the opposite side. For the greatest stretch and strengthening of the muscles, execute with the arms overhead, holding a light weight in the hands for greater resistance if needed. Be sure to keep the arms straight to produce the strongest effect and to shift the hips and shoulders through a full range of motion. This allows you to go through the longest range of motion (see figs. 7.7a–c).

(a)

Figure 7.6 Side bend with hip slide starting position

(b)

Lower shoulders toward dumbbell and shift hips away.

(c)

Lower shoulders right and shift hips toward dumbbell.

Joint Action: Spinal Hyperextension

As you end the shoulder turn in the follow-through, especially after a big swing, you end up in a forward-facing reverse-C curve (a hyperextended spine). In this position, the hips are forward and the shoulders are back so that you can see the letter-C opening to the rear. This position requires a strong eccentric stretch of the abdominals, as well as adequate strength of the erector spinae muscles of the lower back. If you do not have much hip slide and finish in an erect stance, you do not have to do the following exercises.

Yessis Back Machine Sit-Ups

To stretch and strengthen the abdominals, the Yessis Back Machine is used, since this is the only apparatus on which you can assume the correct reverse-C curve position to strengthen the abdominals through the full range of motion. To execute, assume a seated position with the hips directly on the rounded seat when your

(a)

Figure 7.7 Spinal hyperextension

(b)

Stretch to the right to increase abdominal flexibility.

(c)

Stretch to the left for full range of motion.

feet are secured between the rollers. Cross your hands over your chest and then inhale and hold your breath as you slowly lower the body until the trunk is slightly below the level of the hips (see fig. 7.8a).

Do not let your back arch to a great extent so that the head gets close to the floor. The amount of lower back arching should duplicate or go slightly beyond the amount that you exhibit in the follow-through. After reaching the lowermost position, contract the abdominals, and sit up (see fig. 7.8b). Pause momentarily and repeat for the desired number of repetitions. If this exercise seems too difficult, do large ball sit-ups until you feel confident about moving on.

Large Ball Sit-Ups

If a Yessis Back Machine is not available, you can do a similar exercise on a large inflated ball. In this case, you should first assume a seated position on a large ball. Then roll the ball and hips forward as you lie back on the ball. In the final position, the ball supports your

(a)

Figure 7.8　Yessis Back Machine sit-ups starting position

(b)

After reaching the lowermost position, contract the abdominals, and sit up.

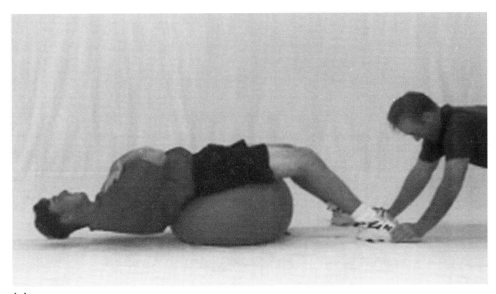

(a)

Figure 7.9 Roll the ball and hips forward as you lie back.

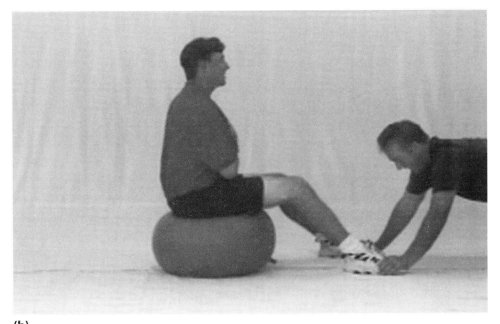

(b)

Have someone hold your feet and sit up.

lower back and you have an arch in your back (see fig. 7.9a). Have someone hold your feet to maintain this position, and then sit up and return to the original position (see fig. 7.9b). This exercise can also be done on a high, sturdy table. Execution is basically the same as on the Yessis Back Machine, except that someone must hold your legs down.

Backward Overhead Medicine Ball Toss

The backward overhead medicine ball toss is an excellent exercise not only for strengthening the lower back, but also for using the abdominals to control the amount of the reverse-C curve. It duplicates what you must do in the end position of the swing.

(a)

Figure 7.10 Backward overhead medicine ball toss starting position.

(b)

Extend the trunk and legs while you keep the arms straight, raise the ball, and release it overhead.

To execute, assume a standing position as in the golf stance, holding a ball in arms extended in front of the body. Legs should be slightly flexed, and the trunk should be inclined forward, while still maintaining the normal curvature of the spine. When ready, go into a squat (see fig. 7.10a) and then inhale and hold your breath as you extend the trunk and legs. At the same time, keep the arms straight, raise the ball up, and release it overhead as the body is fully extended and as you go into the reverse-C curve (see fig. 7.10b). Toss the ball easily in the early stages. When you master this exercise and develop the technique, strength, and flexibility you need, you can throw the ball for maximum height and distance to the rear.

By doing these specialized strength and flexibility exercises, you will enhance the follow-through, which is so critical for maximum explosive force. In addition, you will have a smooth, fluid swing, greater accuracy of ball contact, and a balanced finish position.

8

Combination Exercises

Developing Combination Exercises

The exercises described in the preceding chapters develop strength and flexibility in specific movements and phases of the swing. It is also valuable to do exercises that combine two or more actions in the same or different phases of the swing. For example, execution of weight shift and hip and shoulder rotation can be combined into one exercise focusing on one phase of the swing. You can also combine elements of the backswing, downswing, and follow-through into one exercise.

Using Training Devices

It is possible to execute combined movements with the aid of special training devices.

Medicine Ball

Consider the benefits of using a medicine (weighted) ball during combined exercises. Medicine balls are very effective in developing strength, flexibility,

and power not only in an isolated action, but in movements that duplicate several sequential actions in two or more phases of the swing. For example, you can duplicate the hip and shoulder actions in the backswing, downswing, and follow-through. Because of the resistance provided by the ball's weight, you gain greater strength of the muscle groups used while executing these major actions. In integrating several actions, you also begin to develop a more coordinated and rhythmical swing. Medicine balls are an excellent means of accomplishing both physical conditioning and skill development.

Medicine balls are also quite effective for the development of explosive rotational strength so valuable to golfers—there are no exercises with conventional equipment that can be used for this purpose. In essence, the explosive (speed-strength) muscular development is achieved by executing various types of throws using hip and shoulder rotation with the medicine balls.

Add medicine ball movements to the exercises in this chapter as you work toward achieving a smooth and explosive swing.

The Impact Builder

The Impact Builder can be used to analyze and train specific actions. It is identical to an iron, except for the clubhead. Instead of a hitting surface, it has a cylindrical unit that reacts to centrifugal force. It has adjustable power setting levels to indicate the amount of force generated in the swing. A click sound occurs at the moment the centrifugal force in the swing equals the amount set (see fig. 8.1). To simulate a ball for better duplication of the swing, a 3-D golf ball is used. It is a visual image that is created when you look directly over a special card that shows the image of a ball in three dimensions.

Because of the feedback given by the click sound, you can identify where maximum force is generated. Thus, for example, if you hear the click up around shoulder height, then you know that the arm and wrist action occurred too early. In this case, you should hold the cocked position longer. To help you do this, practice the radial flexion exercise (page 32). You can also emphasize a stronger weight shift and hip rotation before beginning the arm and wrist actions. Do the key exercises for each.

Because the Impact Builder can be used as a diagnostic or training tool, it can help you analyze and perfect your swing. Once a problem area is identified, you can then do the individual or combination exercises needed to improve the actions and to develop the new neuromuscular pathway needed. For example, as you develop the muscles involved in the wrist break, you also develop a muscle memory to ensure that ulnar flexion and arm rotation occur after the shoulder turn and arm actions.

This training can also be done together with an assist from the Active Cords or against the resistance of the Active Cords.

Active Cords

You may choose to add Active Cords to your combined exercises. The Active Cords set consists of a special nonslip hip belt, three differently tensioned elastic tubes, two handles, an ankle strap, and a dual attachment strap. It provides for a variety of different actions that can be done individually or com-

Figure 8.1   The Impact Builder

bined into an integrated movement. The tubing can be attached to different spots on the hip belt and the exercises done against the resistance of the cords. Resistance is provided in the stretching of the tubing. The greater the stretch or the more cords that are combined in one movement, the greater the resistance. The Active Cords provide assistance when the movement is executed with the return of the tubing to its original state. (The stretched tubing pulls the body part exercised back to its original shape with increasing speed.)

The Active Cords can also be used with the medicine ball and Impact Builder. Most important, the Active Cords allow you to execute movements that duplicate the entire swing or portions of it. They are very beneficial in not only learning a good swing but in making corrections and enhancing the strength of the muscles for a more powerful swing.

Weighted Pants

Another effective way to combine resistance training with the total swing is to use weighted pants. The weights, which are distributed around the thighs, allow you to execute the golf swing in the same manner but with additional resistance in the lower body.

Figure 8.2 Weighted pants

The weighted pants, such as those by FitStyle, have weights in the front, side, and rear of the pants so that when you execute weight shift and hip rotation, you must use the muscles in a more powerful action than when not wearing the weighted pants. This helps you to emphasize the forward weight shift and hip rotation movements to effectively start the downswing. The weighted pants can also be used to strengthen the legs (especially the hip joint muscles) when you wear them while walking the course or doing various exercises such as the squat or hip adduction and abduction.

Because the weights are located close to the center of gravity of the thighs, they give you greater lower-body stability. They do not produce excessive momentum during your hitting or walking, and they create sufficient resistance to strengthen the muscles in the hips and thighs. If you walk for aerobic fitness, the weighted pants produce a faster and stronger training effect.

If the dress code where you play allows for wearing nonstandard golf clothing, you can even play a round of golf wearing the weighted pants. Some golfers find that the extra weight around the hip–thigh area reminds them to clear the hips first in the swing, which, in turn, improves their swing

greatly. In figure 8.2, you can see the weighted pants being used together with an Impact Builder.

Exercises

The following combination exercises duplicate the major actions and movements that take place during different phases of the swing.

- Weight shift and hip rotation
- Backward and forward hip and shoulder rotation
- Underhand throw
- Sidearm and backward throw
- Explosive catching and throwing

Weight Shift and Hip Rotation

Forward weight shift, followed by the hip turn with some overlap in sequence, is the key to clearing the hips. This makes it possible for the rest of the body movements to take place in an orderly and smooth manner.

The weight shift and hip rotation exercise with the elastic cords will train you to transfer weight and rotate the hips prior to shoulder rotation. To do this exercise, attach one end of the cord to the belt buckle behind the right hip. The tubing should then wrap around the right hip and go across the front of the body on its way to being secured hip-high. Be sure that there is tension in the tubing before you begin and that the belt is secured snugly around the hips, not the waist.

Take a short backswing to increase the tension of the cord around the hips (see fig. 8.3a). After this, shift the hips forward and allow the tubing to give you an assist in quickly rotating the hips (see fig. 8.3b).

In this exercise, the elastic cord pulls the hips to give you a faster and earlier hip turn. As you do this movement, hold the shoulders back until the hips have rotated. This separation of hip and shoulder rotation creates greater force in the hit. Golfers who do this exercise maintain that it may be the best exercise for not only learning but also enhancing the clearing of the hips.

To develop greater strength of the hip muscles, instead of attaching the Active Cord behind the right

(a)

Figure 8.3 Take a short backswing.

(b)

Allow the tubing to help you quickly rotate the hips.

hip, attach it to the side of the right hip. The cord should then be on a straight line with the stationary attachment. When you are ready, execute weight shift and then rotate the hips forward. As you do this, there will be increased tension on the cord, which will develop greater strength of the muscles involved in not only weight shift but in hip rotation (see figs. 8.4a–b).

A medicine ball may also be introduced into this exercise. Attach the Active Cord to the side of the right

hip and stand sideways to the attachment. Hold a medicine ball in both hands so that you have the resistance of not only the tubing but the medicine ball. Hold the medicine ball in both hands together with the tensed rubber tubing attached to the hips (see fig. 8.5a).

When you are ready, take a backswing (see fig. 8.5b) and then push the hips (weight) forward. Next, rotate the hips to increase the muscle tension (see fig. 8.5c). Rotate the shoulders to bring the ball across the body

(a)

Figure 8.4 Active Cord is attached to the side of the right hip.

(b)

Execute weight shift then rotate the hips forward.

until both hands are on the left side of the body (see fig. 8.5d). Return to the initial position and repeat. When this exercise is mastered, you will be ready to release. Also, you should now be able to demonstrate greater speed of movement for all the actions in sequence.

As you do this exercise, you should feel the built-up tension in the muscles prior to letting go of the med-

icine ball. This is effective for letting you know that you have cleared the hips, which in turn will increase speed of the arms through the hitting area. After you have mastered these actions with the Active Cords, remove the belt and do the same exercise with only the medicine ball or with no resistance. You will experience an easier and faster clearing of the hips.

(a)

Figure 8.5   Starting position

(b)

Take a backswing.

(c)

Rotate the hips.

(d)

Rotate the shoulders to bring the ball across.

Backward and Forward Hip and Shoulder Rotation

Backward and forward hip and shoulder rotation is effective for strengthening the muscles around the midsection. For example, the abdominal rotational muscles are involved when you rotate forward in a sidearm or underhand motion; the lower back muscles are involved in backward rotation and in holding the normal curvature of the spine. In these hip and shoulder turns with a medicine ball, you imitate the actions used in the golf swing.

To execute the turns with the medicine ball, assume a golf stance holding a weighted ball in extended arms. When ready, rotate backward as though taking the backswing, bringing the ball up and to the rear but not overhead (similar to the movement shown in figs. 8.5a–d). Then shift the weight forward, rotate the hips, and turn the shoulders, bringing the ball forward. Do not release the ball; keep holding it as you turn backward and forward. By doing this, you not only develop the feel for the motion, but also use the muscles in a stopping action, which is very important in the follow-through for the prevention of injury.

To be sure that the exercise is done correctly and safely, do not use an extremely heavy ball. Usually anywhere from six to ten pounds is sufficient. Also, do not rotate and swing the arms very forcefully. This will make the stopping action more difficult and may cause injury. Execute at a slow to moderate rate of speed. Keep in mind that the main reason for doing this exercise is to develop the rhythm and feel of the swing while taxing the muscles.

Underhand Throw

To execute, hold a ball weighing approximately four to ten pounds in both hands while in the golf stance. (The exact ball weight depends on your physical abilities.) Rotate the shoulders to the rear as in the backswing. If you take a sufficiently long backswing, there will also be some hip rotation to the rear (see fig. 8.6a). When the trunk is rotated back, shift your weight forward and then rotate the hips and shoulders forward to release the ball.

In initial stages, hold the medicine ball in extended arms as you execute the backswing, downswing, and follow-through. Keep the movements relatively slow and concentrate on developing the rhythm of the movement. Throw the ball in an underhand motion to a partner, or against a rebounding surface if practicing by yourself (see fig. 8.6b). After catching the ball on the return, stop and prepare for another throw.

(a)

Figure 8.6 Underhand throw starting position

(b)

Throw the ball in an underhand motion.

(a)

Figure 8.7   Underhand throw with Active Cords

(b)

Throw the ball in an underhand motion.

The exercise can also be performed with Active Cords (see figs. 8.7a–b).

Since the medicine balls are weighted, your muscles must work harder in these actions. As a result, you strengthen the leg, hip, lower back, and abdominal muscles involved in weight shift and in hip and shoulder rotation. It should be noted that even though the balls provide resistance, they do not interfere with your swing mechanics. The muscles of your midsection and hips are large and strong and they can handle heavier weights without detracting from the fine points of the swing.

Even though the medicine ball can be somewhat heavy, it stays relatively close to the body during the swing action. If you instead swing a golf club weighted at the clubhead, much greater forces can be created in the swing even though the weight is less than that of the medicine ball. As a result, there is greater stress on the shoulders, arms, and wrists when using a golf club weighted at the end, but not on the midsection muscles. Because of this, you should not use a very heavy weighted club. In addition, a heavy clubhead can interfere greatly with the neuromuscular patterning involved—that is, you cannot duplicate the exact actions of the trunk, arms, and hands.

Sidearm and Backward Throw

The sidearm pattern (similar to the baseball swing) does not duplicate the true movement pattern of the golf swing. It does, however, involve the hip and shoulder rotation in basically the same manner. Thus, by doing hip and shoulder rotation while in a relatively upright position, you can strengthen the muscles involved in weight shift and hip and shoulder rotation in the backswing, downswing, and follow-through. To make the movement closer to the actual golf swing, use an underhand-sidearm ball throw.

To execute, assume a side-facing position to a partner. Hold a medicine ball weighing approximately six to ten pounds in both hands directly in front of the body in extended arms about hip- to waist-high (see fig. 8.8a). When ready, inhale and hold your breath as you rotate the shoulders as in the backswing. Then shift your weight forward and rotate the hips and shoulders as in the downswing. Release the ball and go into the follow-through (see figs. 8.8b–c). In this exercise, you execute the hip and shoulder actions involved in the swing. The arms should work together with the shoulders so

(a)

Figure 8.8 Sidearm throw starting position

(b)

Rotate the shoulders as in the backswing.

(c)

Shift your weight forward and rotate the hips and shoulders. Release the ball and follow through.

that after the arms release the ball, the arms move upward as the shoulders go into the follow-through. Do not use this exercise to strengthen the arm action in the swing. It is appropriate only for mid-section development.

When using the underhand and underhand/sidearm patterns, be sure that you maintain an erect (but slightly inclined) trunk with the lower back held in its normal, slightly arched position at all times. If the ball comes to you at an awkward angle and you must reach or stretch to catch it, do not attempt to take a back-swing and throw at the same time. Do this only when you have a good return and can use the same rhythm and body movement pattern for the catching and throwing motion. Follow the ball as it leaves your hands the same as after hitting a golf ball. Doing this will result in greater consistency, which will transfer to the actual swing.

To use the backward throw pattern, assume the same golf stance, holding the ball in extended arms, with the feet shoulder-width apart and the lower body stable (see fig. 8.9a). When ready, inhale and hold your breath, then raise the trunk and rotate the shoulders to the right and throw the ball to the rear (see fig. 8.9b). Use an underhand motion so that when you release the ball the hands are shoulder-high or above. This is a great exercise not only for strengthening the lower back muscles, but also for achieving a full shoulder turn in the backswing.

Explosive Catching and Throwing

A variant of the underhand sidearm throw is to throw and catch in an explosive manner with a partner. Stand in a side-facing position so that your left shoulder is in line with the left shoulder of your partner. Stand approximately 8 to 10 feet apart. When you are ready, toss the ball in front of your partner so that he can catch it with extended arms, bring it back as in the backswing, and then throw it to you quickly with hip and shoulder rotation (see fig. 8.10). As soon as you catch the ball, quickly rotate the hips and shoulders as a unit (or only the shoulders) back as in the backswing, and then rotate the hips and shoulders as a unit (or only the shoulders) forward to release the

(a)

Figure 8.9 Backward throw starting position

(b)

Raise the trunk, rotate the shoulders right, and throw the ball to the rear.

Figure 8.10 Explosive catching and throwing

ball as quickly as possible. Emphasize either the hip or shoulder turn.

The key to successfully doing this exercise is to isolate movement and to quickly return the ball soon after receiving it. This develops the ability to explosively whip the hips or shoulders around (to improve their force-producing actions). However, do not do this exercise to the exclusion of the other exercises that more closely duplicate the entire swing. This exercise is used mainly for hip or shoulder rotation, which must then be incorporated into the total swing.

Note: To prevent injury, it is important that you do not do any medicine ball or Active Cord exercises when you are fatigued. When the muscles are tired, you may not, for example, be able to hold the spine in its normal position. In addition, fatigue changes how you throw and catch the ball and how you do various exercises. This, in turn, may change the neuromuscular patterning that you are developing. When technique work is done together with strength and flexibility development, you should always be in a fresh, energetic state.

9

Troubleshooting the Golf Swing

Identifying Common Problems with the Swing

Most golfers know about the basic actions that comprise a good swing. But even with this knowledge, you may still have difficulty in executing the key actions and in learning new techniques. You may think that you need more practice, but even this may not work if you do not have the strength and flexibility to execute the movements.

For example, I recently worked with a golfer who had a fair understanding of the separation between the hips and shoulders (the X-factor). He was positive that his hips rotated through prior to shoulder rotation in the downswing. However, as we looked at his golf swing tape frame by frame, I pointed out how the hips and shoulders rotated together as a unit. I then asked him to execute forward hip rotation while keeping the shoulders in a side-facing position. He could not do it!

As soon as the hips began to rotate, the shoulders also went into rotation. In essence, his trunk worked as a unit and there was no separation between the hips and shoulders. He was unable to execute one movement without the other. Even though he wanted to separate hip and shoulder rotation, he was unable to execute the movements. When I tested his flexibility with the reverse trunk twist exercise, the reasons became clear: he lacked midsection flexibility, and the rotational abdominal muscles were extremely weak.

Using Specialized Exercises to Correct Your Swing

To assist you in improving your swing, I have identified some of the more common problems and how they can be corrected with special exercises. As you master the exercise, you will also develop the muscular feel of this movement. This in turn will allow you to duplicate the movement in the total swing and to execute it well. You will feel the action when you incorporate it into the other movements that are already strongly ingrained. In this way, the specialized exercise can alleviate the problem that you are having and allow you to hit with consistency and accuracy.

Common Problems—Effective Solutions

Problem: Inability to transfer weight (execute weight shift)

Sliding the hips toward the target (weight shift) is very important for initiating the downswing. When the weight is shifted onto the forward leg, it sets up a new axis of rotation for the hips and shoulders that can create more force. The key joint action for weight shift is hip abduction.

Solution: Hip abduction (hip slide)

When doing hip abduction with rubber tubing, contract the muscles on the right side of the hips to push the hips against the tubing resistance. This forces you to move (slide) the hips over the left (forward) leg to transfer weight. The key to effective execution is to feel the hips, and only the hips, moving toward the target before hip rotation begins. (See page 39 for details.)

Problem: Inability to clear (rotate) the hips early

Forward rotation of the hips prior to shoulder rotation is very important for not only generation of explosive force, but for ensuring a smooth, effortless, and safe swing. Without early hip rotation it is impossible to separate the hip and shoulder turns, which may set you up for back injury!

Solution: Hip rotation with resistance

The key exercise to develop a feel for hip rotation (after weight shift) is hip rotation against the resistance of an Active Cord. After weight transfer, rotate the hips a full 90 degrees while maintaining the shoulders in a side-facing position. Isolate the action to include only the hips. In addition, you can execute weight shift with hip rotation using a medicine ball.

These exercises develop the muscle feel involved in leading with and clearing the hips. The more the movement is isolated to the hips, the greater the force that can be generated when the shoulders rotate. For more details on the hip rotation and combined weight shift and hip rotation exercises, see pages 40 and 71, respectively. If you do not have the necessary midsection flexibility, do the reverse trunk twist first (see page 42 for details).

Problem: Slicing the ball

Regardless of the type of swing you have, the main reason a slice occurs is that you have an open clubface during contact. This puts sidespin on the ball, causing it to break right.

Solution: Left arm lateral and right arm medial rotation

To correct a slice, it is important to bring the clubhead back to the square position by fully turning the arms (an action that also develops greater force). The best exercises to strengthen the muscles involved are medial and lateral arm rotation with the Strength Bar. Do the exercises with both arms. These exercises are described on page 52.

If you have bent arms when you make contact with the ball, then you should also do the supination and pronation exercise with the Strength Bar (see page 49). However, it should be noted that this hand action is much more difficult to control than lateral and medial rotation of the arms. Thus I strongly recommend you modify your technique to do arm rotation rather than relying on left hand supination and right hand pronation to return the clubhead to the square position.

Problem: Early wrist break (casting)

When an early wrist break occurs, most of the force generated in the clubhead is expended prior to contact with the ball. This results in a loss of valuable distance.

Solution: Radial flexion with Strength Bar

To correct an early wrist break, it is important to maintain the cocked wrist position as long as possible, or at least until the hands approach or are below hip level. One of the best exercises to help you hold the cocked position is radial flexion with the Strength Bar. This exercise is described on page 32.

Another valuable exercise is executing the golf swing with the Impact Builder. The Impact Builder lets you know where the wrist break occurred by giving you feedback via a click sound at the point of reaching maximum clubhead speed. For example, if you hear the click when the arms are level with the shoulders during the downswing, then you know that the wrists broke too early. When you hear the click at the impact position (clubhead between the feet), then you know the wrist break occurred at the right time. Use the feedback to determine which exercise is most needed.

Problem: Inability to maintain balance during or after the swing

Balance during the swing, as well as in the follow-through, is very important to ensure a full, smooth swing that generates explosive force at impact. It indicates effective execution of the actions involved.

Solution: Hip abduction and squat

To maintain a stable position during the swing, it is important to strengthen the muscles on the sides of the hips, as well as the muscles of the thigh, to hold the legs in place. The best exercises to develop the strength of the legs as needed to maintain a balanced position are the basic squat and delay squat. They are described on pages 20 and 22, respectively.

To develop the muscles on the sides of the hips, which also drive the hips forward, do hip abduction. This exercise is described on page 39. By executing the hip slide and maintaining a stable leg position, your balance should be enhanced greatly.

Problem: Up-and-down body movement during the swing

This is a very common problem, especially with beginners, who have a tendency to straighten the legs during the backswing and bend the legs during the downswing. (In some cases, it is the reverse.)

Solution: Delay squat and good morning

To eliminate the up-and-down movement, it is necessary to develop ample strength, especially isometric strength of the leg muscles, to hold the lower

body stable. The best exercises to do this are the delay squat and the good morning. They are described on pages 22 and 23, respectively.

You should try to eliminate the up-and-down movement even if you are a consistent hitter. For example, I once played with two elderly ladies who hit the ball well and were very consistent in their hits. However, their up-and-down movements were very visible. If they put more force into their weight shift rather than having the up-and-down movement, they would have been able to hit the ball a good 30 or 40 yards farther. Even when you may have a consistent swing, if you want to increase distance, it is necessary to stabilize the body and to concentrate on the proven force-producing movements.

Problem: Interrupted rhythm, a jerky or broken swing

Overemphasizing a particular body or limb action usually causes an interrupted or broken swing. Such a swing might also be due to not clearing the hips early in the swing or beginning the swing with the arms and then shifting weight backward.

Solution: Medicine ball throws

One of the best exercises to develop a smooth rhythm is to throw a medicine ball in an underhand and underhand/sidearm pattern. These are explained on pages 74–76. When doing these exercises, concentrate on integrating the different actions in sequence—weight shift, hip rotation, shoulder rotation, and arm swing. Do not rely on only the arms or shoulders and arms to throw the ball.

Problem: Inability to get a long and compact backswing

There are three common reasons for not getting a long, compact backswing: 1) insufficient flexibility in the midsection, 2) not being able to get the left arm close to the body, and 3) not holding the rear leg and right shoulder firm so that they become the axis of rotation.

Solution: Reverse trunk twist, shoulder stretch, and static rear leg adduction

To be able to bring the left arm in close to the body you should do the shoulder stretch as described on page 33. It stretches and strengthens the muscles on the back of the shoulder. To create greater midsection rotational flexibility, do the reverse trunk twist. If you have difficulty rotating the shoulders to the rear, the back raise with a twist may be needed. The reverse trunk twist and back raise with a twist are described on pages 42 and 30, respectively.

Shifting too much weight to the rear instead of coiling the upper body can also prevent you from getting a tight, compact backswing position. To prevent this, it is important to strengthen the muscles on the inside of the right thigh with the isometric (static) hip adduction exercise. It is described on page 34. Doing this exercise will help to maintain the right leg in position as you rotate the shoulders to the rear in the early part of the swing.

Problem: Inability to get much separation between hip and shoulder rotation (X-factor)

The key to generating explosive power is to get as much separation as possible between the hip and shoulder rotation early in the downswing. Since weight shift and hip rotation should precede shoulder rotation, the hips should be slightly beyond the address position when the shoulders begin their action.

Solution: Reverse trunk twist

The best exercise to separate the hip and shoulder movements is the reverse trunk twist. This exercise helps to develop the flexibility of the midsection and strength of the abdominal rotational muscles that are used to turn the shoulders forward. This exercise is described on page 42.

Also helpful is the weight shift and hip rotation exercise described on page 71. When you master weight shift and hip rotation (clearing the hips) without involving the shoulders, you will then be able to develop greater separation of the hip and shoulder movements. This will result in much greater force being applied in the hit.

Problem: Hooking the ball

A common reason for hitting a hook is the overpowering of the left hand by the right hand. In essence, the right forearm undergoes excessive pronation as the arm straightens from its bent position in the backswing. There may also be excessive inward rotation of the right arm when it is straightened prior to contact. In some cases, it may be overturning of the left or a combination of these actions.

Solution: Wrist break and arm rotation

I have had success in correcting the hook by using 1) stronger ulnar flexion to place greater emphasis on the wrist break and 2) lateral rotation of the right arm to correct an imbalance between the medial and lateral arm rotator muscles. By strengthening the muscles involved in these actions, you are better able to counteract the tendency of the right hand and arm to overpower the left. (If both arms are bent during contact, then it is necessary to do more supination with the right forearm and pronation with the left.)

Also beneficial in emphasizing the wrist break is use of the Impact Builder. It is very effective not only for feedback on where you generate maximum force, but also in requiring you to execute the wrist action immediately prior to contact in order to elicit the click sound.

Problem: Inability to block the left wrist during impact

If the left wrist extensor muscles are much stronger than the flexors, they may pull the hand into hyperextension, which leads to a scooping action. This results in superfluous movement of the clubhead, which leads to less force and accuracy.

Solution: Wrist exercises

To be able to hold the hand in line with the forearm throughout the contact phase, it is important to have ample isometric wrist strength. To strengthen the muscles as needed, do static wrist flexion and wrist extension with Exer Rings. These exercises are described on page 56.

Problem: Aching lower back muscles after playing a round of golf

Getting a sore lower back during or after finishing 18 holes can be due to excessive muscle fatigue, ineffective technique, or a poor stance. If your stance and technique are good and you clear the hips before the shoulder rotation in your swing, then the problem is usually muscular.

Solution: Good morning and back raise

The best exercises to prevent fatigue of the lower back muscles are the good morning and the back raise. They are described on pages 23 and 91, respectively. The good morning exercise helps you to hold the trunk in proper position during the swing. The back raise is the best exercise to strengthen the lower back muscles through the full range of motion, which then allows them to handle stressful situations well.

Problem: Excessive body fatigue

Overall body fatigue during play and especially after completing a round of golf is fairly common. There are various reasons for this, but most often it involves a lack of cardiorespiratory and strength endurance. It may also be due to poor nutrition.

Solution: Aerobics, endurance training, and smart eating

One of the more effective ways of improving cardiovascular and respiratory endurance is to do aerobic activities such as walking, cycling, swimming, and running. Such activities should be done up to four to five times per week for thirty minutes or more per workout session. With less fatigue, many golfers have seen their games improve noticeably.

Muscular endurance is involved if you are not able to execute the swing in the same manner on every hole, if you begin to lose your feel for the swing, or if the muscles feel tired from the walking and standing. In this case, do the strength exercises for about fifteen to twenty maximum repetitions for the major muscles involved in the golf swing. Fatigue can also be caused by poor nutrition, skipping meals, energy-deficient meals, and poor or inadequate water intake. If fatigue occurs during play, eating a nutritional bar such as the Standard Bar may be beneficial.

Problem: Excessive rolling of the feet

Some golfers are unable to hold the feet in good contact with the ground during the backswing and the downswing. Solid foot contact is especially important in keeping the weight pressed on the inside of the right leg during the backswing in order to get a tight coiling of the upper body. If you find your ankle rolling out to the side, it allows excessive weight to go to the rear, making it more difficult to shift the weight forward to initiate the downswing. There may also be excessive rolling of the forward foot during the downswing that does not allow you to maintain a firm base or axis of rotation.

Solution: Ankle adduction and abduction

To be able to hold the feet in place and to handle the weight that moves on and off the feet, you should do ankle adduction and abduction. These exercises will also help to prevent ankle sprains.

For ankle adduction, assume a seated position on the floor with the Active Cord wrapped around the midfoot. Attach the ends of the rubber tubing to a stationary post or other object. When ready, keep the leg straight and turn the sole of the foot inward against the resistance of the cord. Then turn the sole outward and repeat for the necessary repetitions (see figs. 9.1a–b).

For ankle abduction, assume a seated position as in the ankle adduction exercise, but face the opposite way so that the leg to be exercised is farther away from the attachment. When ready, keep the leg straight and turn the sole of the foot outward as far as possible. Return the foot to an inward position and then repeat (see figs. 9.2a–b).

Problem: Difficulty in holding a firm grip during impact

The force that is generated by the body and transferred to the clubhead can be very high in an explosive swing. If the hit is off-center, by even an eighth of an inch, there is a very strong tendency for the clubhead to turn. If not counteracted by the hand grip, it can lead to poor hits and inaccurate shots.

In addition, in order to transfer the generated forces to the clubhead, it is necessary that the grip be very firm at the moment of impact. If the grip is

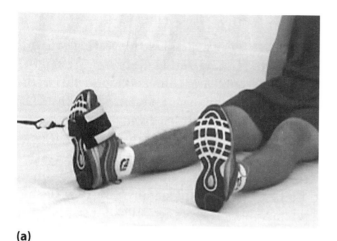

(a)

Figure 9.1 Ankle adduction starting position

relaxed or loose, some of the forces generated will be absorbed, resulting in decreased distance and the possibility of the clubface turning.

Solution: Finger strengthening

To strengthen the grip, you should do finger flexion exercises in both dynamic and static modes. For details on how to do the grip exercises, see pages 54–55.

Problem: Falling or leaning backward after the shot

Having all the weight on the back foot or falling backward after taking a shot is a common fault, especially among senior golfers. There are several reasons for this, which may include: 1) straightening of the front leg that pushes the hips to the rear

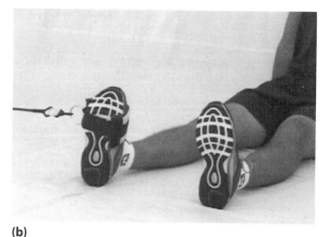

(b)

Turn the foot inward.

during the swing; 2) starting the swing with the arms before involving the hips and shoulders; and 3) not shifting the weight forward at the beginning of the swing. When the weight is shifted onto the front leg and you then execute the hip and shoulder rotation, you not only impart greater force to the ball, but there will not be any backward motion.

Solution: Hip abduction

The hip abduction exercise is described on page 39. Also useful is the weight shift and hip rotation exercise as described on page 71. To correct straightening of the forward leg that drives the hips to the rear during the swing, the basic squat or delay squat is needed to maintain a stable leg position. These exercises are described on pages 20 and 22, respectively.

(a)

Figure 9.2 Ankle abduction starting position

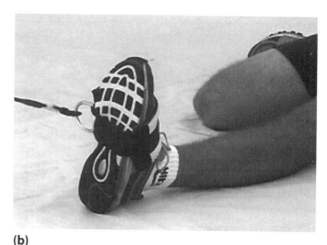

(b)

Turn the foot outward.

CHAPTER

10

Back Strength

The Key to Golf Longevity

Developing a Strong Back

The key to a golfer's ability to play well for many years is a strong back. Back injury is nothing to sneeze at! You can probably imagine, or perhaps you already know, how badly you can hurt your back when swinging the golf club. A bad back can put a crimp in not only your swing, but also in your ability to continue participating in the sport. It can affect you at work, on the dance floor, and even in bed. But you should understand that it is possible to have a strong, supple back for life. Even if you already suffer from back pain, you can do something about it. In this chapter I will show you how, so that you, too, can enjoy golf to its fullest.

The spine, which many golfers tend to think of as the weakest link in the body, is in fact beautifully designed. Back problems arise mainly from abuse. In its normal extended position, the spine and its discs can cope with tremendous loads safely and efficiently. Why then do so many golfers have back problems? I have found that most low back injuries are due to improper back posture in the stance and during the swing. Faulty mechanics and weak muscles also play important roles.

Identifying Back Pain

Poor posture, a major contributor to back pain, often begins in the earliest ages. In school we learn the three Rs, but not how to stand, sit, walk, run, throw, hit, or breathe properly. Because most people take these actions for granted, many poor habits are formed. But learning proper technique is critical to elimination of back pain. For example, poor posture, both static and dynamic, leads to an unnaturally bent spine, resulting in pinched nerve endings that cause low back pain. Back problems can be exacerbated when you are overweight and your abdominal wall protrudes.

Weak musculature usually leads to injury and pain. When the muscles of the back are weak, they cannot hold the spine in proper alignment—and as a result, excessive curvatures occur. They, in turn, allow for higher-than-normal forces to be generated during the swing that cannot be withstood by the spinal support structures. When the weak back muscles cannot withstand the forces produced in the swing, sprains and strains result.

Physicians, as a rule, generally treat the results of back problems, but not the cause. They may treat the pain with aspirin, muscle spasms with ice or heat, and protrusions with traction or surgery, but they do not treat the underlying cause. You will be happy to know, however, that the causes can be uncovered and preventive measures can be taken.

For example, I recently had a golfer call me from another state to tell me that after two weeks his back has never felt so good in over twenty years! He had been to various doctors and had undergone all kinds of therapy, all to no avail. But by doing two simple exercises that I had recommended, he was able to maintain his spine in good alignment and to eliminate the pain that he was experiencing.

Diagnosing Back Injuries

One of the most common injuries to the lower back is a strain (often called a muscle pull). It is usually brought on by a quick movement or a combination of bending and twisting, such as can occur in the golf swing. To prevent such an injury, you must have the normal spinal curve in effect when you twist so that the shearing and compression forces are minimal. When you have a rounded spine and then twist, the shearing and compression forces are very high, and injuries to the discs can easily occur.

Another common problem is *sciatica* (severe pain in the lower back and hip; in severe cases pain is also felt down the leg). Sciatic nerve problems usually result from trauma due to injuries such as lower back sprains, ruptured discs, and poor alignment of the vertebrae. In most cases, putting the spine in proper alignment and strengthening the muscles to hold it in place eliminate sciatica.

A *slipped disc* is a term often used to describe moderate to severe low back pain. But the term is inaccurate, because the disc does not actually slip from between the vertebrae. Instead, it bulges or protrudes from the side when there is weakness in the walls to press on vital nerve roots nearby (also known as a herniated disc). When this happens, the nerve malfunctions; pain, numbness, tingling, and hot and cold sensations begin. In my practice, I have found that most often an exercise program to make the back stronger and more flexible takes care of the

problem (when you are capable of exercising and the amount of herniation is small).

Implementing Back Treatment

Many methods are used to treat back pain, ranging from aspirin to bedrest to yoga and Zen. Spinal manipulation by chiropractors and clinical kinesiologists (advanced chiropractors) can be very helpful. However, in order to maintain the correct alignment after an adjustment, it is important that you strengthen the muscles involved to hold the spine in place. Without such strengthening, your back problem may return.

Massage therapists use different methods to relieve pain, and acupressure, acupuncture, and laser acupuncture are also being used with increasing frequency. Inversion devices in which you hang upside-down or lie in a semi-inverted position are also popular, and some people experience relief. The exact method used usually depends on the doctor treating you.

In many cases, improper strength and flexibility exercises are recommended. For example, the strengthening exercises are usually for the abdominal wall, which does not strengthen the back muscles. For the back muscles, stretching muscles is usually recommended when it is erroneously assumed that the back muscles are already strong and tight.

Doing abdominal exercises for back problems is important because a strong abdominal wall helps to reduce stress on the spine, especially when there is a protruding abdomen. The key to a strong back, however, is strength of the back muscles; the spine must be both flexible and strong. This view is held by most modern back specialists, who believe that the best long-term treatment for back pain is exercise.

Too many back sufferers, however, look to fast relief rather than long-term prevention. Because of this, countless prescriptions are written for medication, repeated back injections are given, and various temporary treatments are used. In such cases, since there are no quick cures, you must learn to live with the problem on a day-to-day basis.

You can, however, overcome most problems with exercise. You must get the midsection (abdominal and lower back) muscles strong and the spine flexible in order to keep the vertebrae in place but apart, so that the discs can fully expand and compress to perform their functions effectively. This will allow you to continue playing golf longer and to swing even more effectively than you did before.

Take the case of Mike, who first came to me in pain and with his back muscles in spasm. He had been to the doctors and they had given him some relief, but he faced surgery. When it was safe, I tested him with various exercises to evaluate the strength and flexibility of his spine. It did not take long to discover that his muscles were extremely weak and that his flexibility was very poor.

I placed him on a program of strength and flexibility exercises that were specific to his problem. The exercises revolved around strengthening the lower back muscles and developing rotational flexibility (two key areas for golfers). After being on the program for a few weeks, he began to see great improvement. He was able to begin swinging a club again, and gradually, as he continued the exercises, he was able to go back to playing. He was thrilled not only with the playing but that he did not experience any pain.

After a few months, even more amazing to Mike (who was fifty-two) was that he was capable of hitting the ball farther than when he was in his twenties! (He had been playing golf for most of his life.) He is just one example of many golfers who have had similar improvement—you can too!

Exercises

Two exercises are recommended to stretch the lower back muscles and connective tissues and to enhance spinal flexibility:

- Full spine inversion
- Supported back stretch

These six exercises are recommended to strengthen the lower back muscles:

- Back raise
- Reverse back raise
- Good morning
- Side bend
- Pelvic thrust
- Cross-body lift

These four exercises are recommended to strengthen the abdominal muscles:

- Reverse trunk twist
- Pelvic tilt
- Reverse sit-up
- 45-degree sit-up (crunch)

These midsection exercises strengthen all the muscles acting on the lumbar spine. This helps greatly in keeping the spinal vertebrae and discs in their natural alignment, especially during the swing. At the same time, your spine will allow movement in all directions so that you can have an explosive swing with maximum safety.

The exercises to be described (especially the back raise and reverse trunk twist exercises) produce excellent results. Back pain is greatly reduced or eliminated, and the number of injuries drops dramatically. In addition, you will have a stronger, injury-proof back. Being a golfer myself, I am sure you can appreciate the benefits of a healthy back, or, more specifically, a strong and healthy midsection, that allows you to have an explosive but smooth and safe swing.

Spinal Flexibility Exercises

In the course of experimenting with exercises designed to improve spinal flexibility, make it a top priority to avoid any activities that involve dangerous stretching. Many exercises recommended to stretch the lower back have great potential for injury. This includes the straight leg toe touch, hurdler's stretch, and variations of the straight leg toe touch such as the alternating straight leg toe touch. The potential danger in these exercises lies in the excessive stretching of the lower back. For example, when you do a straight leg toe touch, when you bend over more than 30 degrees or so, the lower back muscles become inactive. All the stress of supporting the upper body then falls on the lumbar ligaments. By holding the bent-over position for extended periods of time, you then stretch the ligaments, whose main function is to hold the vertebrae and spine in place. As the ligaments become stretched, you in essence develop a looser back that is more prone to injury.

An analogous situation exists with the hurdler stretch and its variants. When you bend over and attempt to touch the toes in a seated position with straight legs, or if you have the legs spread apart and then rotate the spine and bend over to touch the toes of one leg, you excessively stretch the lumbar ligaments. As they become more and more stretched, you develop a very unstable spine that is more prone to injury.

When you hold such extreme positions of the spine (keep in mind that the normal range of motion is approximately 45 degrees of forward flexion and 45 degrees of backward extension), there is also compression on the joint capsules. This in turn presses on the nerve endings and deactivates them so that any pain you might be experiencing is masked. However, once the nerves regain their sensitivity, when the spine is returned to its normal position, the pain comes back.

This is why I strongly recommend active stretches in which the muscles control the range of motion through which you stretch the lower back. This avoids excessive stretching of the lumbar ligaments, and helps you maintain strong support for the back while strengthening the muscles that hold the vertebrae and spine in place.

Full Spine Inversion

In this exercise, you do nothing but hang, relaxed, from the hips. (Hanging from the feet is not recommended because of the excessive pulling on the ankle and knee joints.) Your legs should be in a support position so that only your spine is being stretched. Inversion can be done off a high, sturdy table with someone holding your legs down, on a Yessis Back Machine, or on some of the better inversion devices (see fig. 10.1).

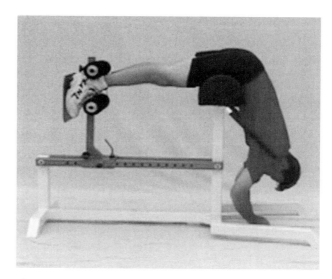

Figure 10.1   Full spine inversion

Supported Back Stretch

Another effective exercise is the supported back stretch using an extremely strong strap that is secured over a door top or around an overhead beam. The handles are situated so that you use a neutral grip—that is, the palms face each other when you grasp the handles approximately chest- or face-high.

To execute, keep your feet in contact with the ground and lower your body into a squat until your arms are fully extended (see fig. 10.2a). Keep your feet on the ground and your back in its natural curvature. As you go down, you will feel a strong stretch in the lower back area. Not only does such hanging stretch the spine, but you stretch the latissimus dorsi muscle, which covers the sides of the lower back area. (Most other back stretches do not affect this muscle.) After pausing momentarily in the down position, rise up, pulling with your arms and pushing with the legs.

If you have a back problem, lower yourself, but move the hips to the rear while you hold the lumbar spine in its normal, slightly arched position as you assume a seated position (see fig. 10.2b). Doing this helps to "unlock" the spine; then, as it becomes looser, you will be able to do the full stretch. For a very full stretch, grasp the handles and lower your body until the hips are lower than the knees. This is a great way to start and end the day (see fig. 10.2c).

Flexibility by itself is not the most important factor in the prevention of injuries. In fact, if you do static

(a)

Figure 10.2   Supported back stretch

(b)

If you have a back problem

(c)

A very full stretch

stretching to develop flexibility, you may create weaker joints, which are even more susceptible to injury! Strength is a key factor in the prevention of injury, along with functional flexibility in which the muscles are actively involved. To develop functional flexibility, the exercises must be done actively and with additional resistance to gain flexibility and strength simultaneously. When strength is coupled with active flexibility, static and active postures are easier to maintain, and the movements involved in the golf swing are enhanced considerably.

For example, if you have tight hip extensor muscles or weak lower back muscles, it will be difficult for you to bend forward while maintaining the normal curvature of the spine. As a result, your spine will usually become rounded, creating greater pressure on the anterior aspects of the discs. When you then swing,

nerve pinching or even disc rupture can occur when the forces are sufficiently great.

Lower Back Strength

To strengthen your lower back muscles to not only prevent injury but to improve your swing, you must strengthen mainly the erector spinae muscle group, which runs the length of the back on both sides of the spine. Also important is strengthening the relatively short and thin deep posterior spinal muscles. They not only help hold the vertebrae in place, but are also involved in various movements of the spine. Last, but equally important, is strengthening the quadratus lumborum for lateral stability of the spine.

In the following exercises, the movements should be performed at a moderate or, in some cases, slow speed. Start with light or no resistance, and increase the resistance or speed of execution only after you master the exercise. The exercises should be done only if you have no medical problems that prevent you from exercising the spinal muscles.

Back Raise

The back raise is the most effective exercise you can do to strengthen the lower back muscles through a full range of motion. Once strengthened, they will be able to easily hold the needed natural curvature of the spine and help to prevent low back muscle fatigue, strains, and other problems. As an added benefit, you will have an erect trunk position for good posture.

For best results, do the back raise on a Yessis Back Machine. Lie facedown on the apparatus so that your pelvic girdle is in full support on the seat when your feet are placed between the rear pads. Hang over from the waist as far as possible (about 50 to 60 degrees down) and relax (see fig. 10.3a). This is the active stretching phase.

When ready, inhale slightly more than usual and raise your trunk until it is above horizontal. You should have a slight arch in the lower back (see fig. 10.3b). Exhale as you return to the down position, pause momentarily, and then repeat. Hold the top position for one or two seconds if you want greater stability of the spine.

If a Yessis Back Machine is not available, the exercise can be done on a high, sturdy table. Position yourself so that your pelvic girdle is in full support on the end of the table (navel at the edge). Place a small rolled-up towel under the lower abdomen to help create greater intraabdominal pressure. (On the Yessis Back Machine, the rounded seat creates the necessary pressure.) To be held in position, you must have someone lie on your legs to hold them down. Execute as described previously.

(a)

Figure 10.3 Back raise active stretch

(b)

Raise your trunk above horizontal.

Reverse Back Raise

If you are uncomfortable hanging down headfirst, you can do the reverse back raise. Lie on the Yessis Back Machine the opposite way so that your pelvis and legs hang down over the seat while you hold onto the rollers or the back plate to stabilize the upper body. The upper abdomen (stomach area) should be over the seat so that your hips are lowered together with the legs (see fig. 10.4a). When ready, inhale and hold your breath as you tilt the hips and raise the legs upward until they are above level (see fig. 10.4b). Exhale as you return to the initial position, relax, and repeat.

(a)

Figure 10.4   Reverse back raise starting position

(b)

Raise the legs higher than level.

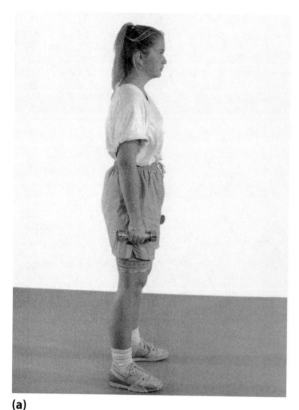

(a)

Figure 10.5   Good morning starting position

(b)

Hold the normal curvature of the back as you bend from the hips.

Good Morning

Although this exercise is explained in Chapter 4, I repeat it here because it is the most important exercise you can do to maintain a proper stance with correct spinal posture during the swing. To execute, stand erect with the feet shoulder-width apart (see fig. 10.5a). Hold the normal curvature in the lower back, and then inhale and bend over from the hips until the trunk is about 45 or more degrees forward (see fig. 10.5b). Hold for three or four seconds, and then return to the initial position. Relax and then repeat. When you can do the exercise comfortably, hold dumbbells in the hands for greater resistance.

Side Bend

The side bend is the only exercise that strengthens the quadratus lumborum, a deep muscle on both sides of the lumbar spine. It is responsible for lateral

stability of the spine, and it is involved in every swing for distance. When one side is weak, you may find your spine curved to the other side (scoliosis). In addition, the quadratus lumborum is involved in many, if not most, back problems, and is thus very important for golfers. (See Chapter 7 for more details.)

To execute the side bend, place one end of the Active Cord under the feet so that it is well secured and so that the tension is relatively great when you are in an erect standing position. When ready, lean toward the side of the tubing so that the tension is reduced. Inhale and hold your breath as you rise up and over to the other side as far as possible (see fig. 10.6a–b). Return to the starting position, then repeat.

Pelvic Thrust

One of the simplest exercises to strengthen the erector spinae muscle through a short range of motion is the pelvic thrust. To execute, lie on your back with

(a)

Figure 10.6   Side bend starting position

(b)

Lean toward the tubing, then rise up and over to the other side.

your knees bent, feet flat on the floor and arms along-side the body (see fig. 10.7a). When you are ready, raise your pelvis until there is a slight arch in the lower back or until you can draw a straight line from the knees to the shoulders (see fig. 10.7b). Return to the initial position and repeat.

Cross-Body Lift

The cross-body lift is a good exercise to develop sta-bility of the lower spine. To execute, assume an all-fours facedown position so that your thighs, arms, and trunk make a rectangle (see fig. 10.8a). When ready, inhale slightly more than usual and hold your breath as you lift one arm and the opposite leg. Raise them until they are in line with or slightly above the spine (see fig. 10.8b). After reaching this

up position and holding for two or three seconds, lower the arm and leg and then repeat with the opposite arm and leg. Exhale as you lower the arm and leg and relax momentarily. Repeat in an alter-nating manner.

Abdominal Exercises

The key to a strong and healthy lumbar spine is to develop a muscular corset around the waist. Having very strong back muscles but very weak abdominal muscles (or vice versa) creates a muscular imbalance that may set you up for back problems. Most effec-tive is to strengthen all the back and abdominal muscles.

(a)

Figure 10.7   Pelvic thrust starting position

(b)

Raise your pelvis until there is a slight arch in the lower back.

(a)

Figure 10.8 Cross-body lift starting position

(b)

Alternate lifting one arm and the opposite leg.

Reverse Trunk Twist

The reverse trunk twist is one of the most important abdominal and lower back exercises that you can do. This exercise not only strengthens the abdominal oblique muscles, but it stretches the back in a rotational action to produce midsection flexibility. It is a must for maximizing hitting distance because it increases the power produced by shoulder rotation in the downswing. The reverse trunk twist also plays a key role in the prevention of injury to the lower back, especially when doing twisting movements.

As brought out in Chapter 6, where the exercise is explained in detail, for best results, it is important that your shoulders maintain contact with the floor as the legs are lowered to one side and then the other. Try to work up to where you can do the exercise with only slightly bent legs in order to have greater resistance for more strength and flexibility development (see figs. 10.9a–c).

Pelvic Tilt

The pelvic tilt is needed only if you have excessive curvature of the lower spine (swayback). To do the pelvic tilt, lie on the floor with your arms at your sides and your legs fully extended (see fig. 10.10a). The position in the figure is somewhat exaggerated so that you can see the curvature of the lower back when you lie on your back.

When you are ready, strongly contract the abdominal muscles and push the lower spine against the floor, rotating the upper pelvis backward (see fig. 10.10b). This exercise will shorten and strengthen the abdominal muscles. In time, the muscles will then hold the pelvic girdle in a more rearward position, eliminating some of the excessive arch. This exercise can also be done while you are in a seated or standing position, though execution in these positions is more difficult.

(a)

Figure 10.9 Reverse trunk twist starting position

(b)

Outside of the foot (or knee) touches the floor.

(c)

Shoulders remain in contact with the floor.

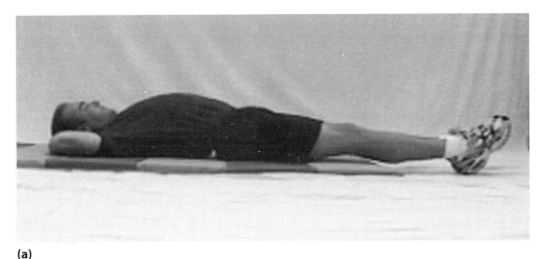

(a)

Figure 10.10   Pelvic tilt starting position (exaggerated arch)

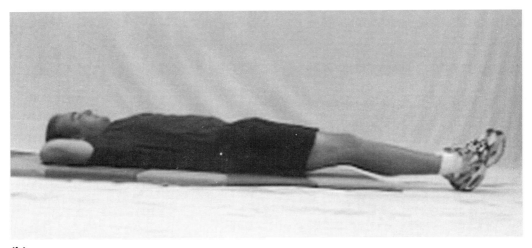

(b)

Contract the abdominal muscles and push the lower spine to the floor.

Reverse Sit-Up

This exercise is important for developing the lower portion of the abdominals. To execute, lie on your back with your knees bent, feet off the floor and thighs perpendicular to the trunk. Keep your arms alongside the body with the palms down (see fig. 10.11a).

When ready, rotate your pelvic girdle and knees up toward the chest (see fig. 10.11b). Be sure that the pelvic girdle is rotated off the floor. If needed, press down with the hands to help get the pelvis up and over. When this version of the exercise becomes easy, place the arms overhead to isolate the lower abdominals (see fig. 10.11c). Note that when you do this exercise, you are also stretching the lower back as in the knee-to-chest stretch.

(a)

Figure 10.11   Reverse sit-up starting position

(b)

Rotate the pelvis and knees toward the chest.

(c)

Advanced arm position isolates the lower abdominals.

45-Degree Sit-Up (Crunch)

The sit-up or crunch develops the upper portion of the abdominal musculature, which plays a role in the follow-through but not in the downswing. To execute, lie on your back, with the arms alongside the body or crossed on your chest (if advanced). The knees should be bent with the feet flat on the floor (see fig. 10.12a).

Inhale and hold your breath as you raise your head and shoulders to about a 45-degree angle. Allow the arms to rise naturally (see fig. 10.12b) or if advanced, keep them folded at the chest. Exhale as you return to the beginning position with the head on the floor. Pause and then repeat. If needed, someone may hold your feet down. When execution becomes easy, cross your hands to increase the resistance.

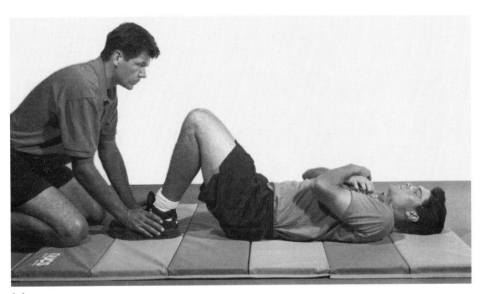

(a)

Figure 10.12   45-degree sit-up starting position (advanced)

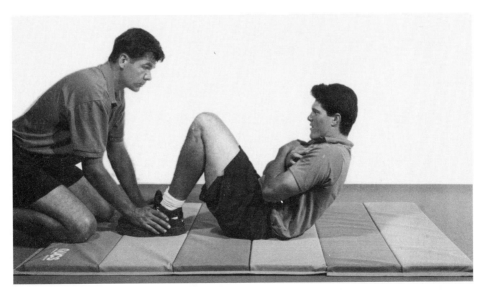

(b)

Raise head and shoulders to about 45 degrees.

Adopting an Exercise Program

Strengthening the lower back and abdominal muscles can take place on a daily basis with one day of rest per week, or on alternate days with a day of rest in-between. If you like to work out every day, do one set of a key exercise for fifteen to thirty repetitions. For example, on one day you may do the side bend and the reverse trunk twist (in the twenty to thirty repetition range), and then finish with one set of twenty to thirty back raises. On the next day you may do the back stretch, reverse sit-up, and twenty or more repetitions of the reverse back raises. This order in exercise execution is repeated throughout the week, and on some days there can be a switch to a different exercise for more variety.

If you prefer working out three times per week, do one or two back and abdominal exercises after doing inversion or the back stretch. You will typically do one or two sets of each exercise for approximately twenty repetitions. Additional resistance can be used for greater strength, or the number of repetitions can be higher for more muscular endurance.

Each of these workout routines is beneficial and can keep your lower back healthy and problem free. Experiment with both routines to see which one fits you best. Most important is that you do the key exercises a minimum of two to three times per week. This includes the back raise or the reverse back raise,

the side bend, and the reverse trunk twist. These should never be omitted. Alternate the other exercises for variety. In this way, you will get the greatest benefits in relation to not only your lower back health and safety, but to enhancing your golf swing and score.

Your program can also include supplementary devices such as a large inflated ball and tush cush, which are beneficial in helping to prevent back problems. When seated on a large inflated ball (approximately twenty-six inches in diameter), your hips tilt forward slightly extending the spine and enabling it to regain its natural curve. When you sit in this position, you can do easy bouncing actions while keeping the feet in contact with the floor and using the back muscles to hold the spine erect. You can also do other exercises such as sit-ups (see page 65) and back arches with these large balls.

The tush cush is a simple device that I recommend when you must sit for long periods (as in driving or working at a desk). It is an angled cushion with an opening in the middle of the back. The tail bone sits in the opening so that no pressure is placed on the spine. The slope of the cushion causes the pelvis to tilt forward slightly to maintain the normal curvature of the spine, which reduces compression forces on the disk.

For more information on designing your exercise program, see Chapter 13.

CHAPTER
11

Warm-Up
Preparing the Muscles for Play

Tuning Up

Before teeing off, most golfers do a variety of movements to loosen up. Some begin swinging easy and gradually build up to full speed. Others do some static stretches and then start swinging, while some do combinations of these. Warm-up is very individualistic; only you know when you are ready.

For greatest accuracy and power in your first few hits and to prevent injury, I strongly recommend that you do some active stretches to prepare the muscles for action. After active stretches and some easy swings, you will be ready to take some full-power practice swings to regroove your neuromuscular memory pathway.

Static Stretching

Most of you are probably familiar with the static stretches that are typically recommended for golf. In these stretches, you hold a particular position (usually at the end of your full range of motion) for up to thirty seconds. During this time, you relax the muscles so that you can increase the range of

motion, but not to a point where it's painful. Doing such static stretching after playing golf is valuable as it helps to relax the muscles and to remove the tension that builds up during play.

I do not, however, recommend doing static stretches before playing. The reason for this is that when you do static stretching, the muscles must already be warmed up and must be very relaxed! In essence, you must "put the muscles to sleep" in order to stretch the connective tissue and muscle fibers to get the full range of motion in the joint. If you then start taking some vigorous swings with the club, you will find that the muscles are not prepared to execute a forceful swing, and may be injured if the forces are sufficiently great. However, if you feel that static stretches benefit you, then do them at least a half-hour before starting to play.

Active Stretching

Active stretches use the muscles dynamically not only to increase flexibility, but to warm up and prepare the muscles for swinging the club (as opposed to being put to "sleep" in the static regimen). Active stretching means that you contract the muscles to move the limbs through the range of motion needed. In this way you actively "turn on" the muscles to be used so that they can act and feel as needed in the swing. At the same time, you stretch the muscles and connective tissue around the joints so that you attain functional flexibility.

It is important to understand that the joint ranges of motion seen in the golf swing are determined by how strongly the muscles contract to move the body and limbs through the needed range of motion. Thus, an active and functional range is determined by the strength of the muscles involved and only partially by the amount of flexibility that you have. In addition, passive flexibility, developed by doing passive static stretches, shows a very low correlation to active flexibility. Active stretches, however, have a very high correlation and actively prepare the muscles for action and help to prevent injury.

In the golf swing, the nervous system must activate the muscles at the right time to move the body and limbs as needed. However, in static stretching, the nervous system is "knocked out" so that it cannot activate the muscles to ensure adequate stretching. However, active stretches involve the neuromuscular system, which helps to duplicate more closely what occurs in the golf swing.

From my analysis of the golf swing, I have come up with ten active stretches that prepare the major muscles involved in the swing. After you do them, you will feel how they improve your swing when first starting. As a result, you will want to incorporate them into your prestart routine right on the golf course.

Doing these exercises enables you to have more effective shots on the first few holes. Too often, golfers are halfway through the round before they truly feel loose and can swing with full power, smoothness, and accuracy. However, by doing these simple exercises before playing, you should be able to start with your best swing.

The active stretches that I recommend prior to playing are based on the same concepts as in the exercises you did in the previous chapters. The only difference is that you are not using any resistance since you only want to warm up and tune up the muscles. Without the added resistance, the exercise becomes a pure stretch and activator of the muscles.

In active stretches, the muscles are responsible for performing the movement and undergo an active stretch during their contraction. Because the muscles are working, they generate heat and warm up the joint, thus preparing the muscles and joints to perform as needed in the swing.

Exercises

The following active stretch exercises are recommended prior to play in order to adequately stretch and prepare those muscles groups that are important to the swing.

- Basic squat
- Lateral arm raise
- Side stretch
- Hip and side stretch
- Twisting
- Rotator cuff stretch
- Protraction and retraction
- Shrug
- Good morning
- Shoulder circles

After you have completed these active stretches, begin to swing the club in an easy manner and gradually build up to your normal swing. To get feedback on how effectively you are swinging and where you are generating maximum force (maximum clubhead speed), swing the Impact Builder. It feels the same as swinging a regular club, but produces a click at the point of maximum force production in your swing. When you feel your swing grooved in with maximum clubhead speed generated at ball contact, you are ready to start playing.

Basic Squat

This exercise is needed to loosen up and prepare the leg muscles, especially the anterior thigh muscles, which play the major role in holding your lower body stable. The legs should feel springy and ready to react to your upper-body movements.

Stand with your feet in the same position as you use for a typical tee shot, and bend your knees to lower the

(a)

Figure 11.1 Basic squat starting position

(b)

Bend the knees to lower the body while keeping the normal curvature of the spine.

body. Keep your spine in its normal curvature and your heels on the ground. After reaching the bottom position, rise up and repeat (see figs. 11.1a–b). Execute for three to five repetitions. (Refer to Chapter 4 for more information on the squat exercise.)

Lateral Arm Raise

An excellent exercise to loosen up the shoulders and to move the scapula through a full range of motion is the lateral arm raise. Begin in a standing position with your arms alongside your body (see fig. 11.2a). Keep your arms straight and raise them out to the sides and overhead as high as possible (see fig. 11.2b). The greater the height, the greater the stretch in the shoulder joints. Return the arms under control to your sides, pause momentarily, and then repeat for three to five repetitions.

Side Stretch

To stretch the midsection and hips in a sideward motion (which is needed for weight shift and a full follow-through), do the side stretch. Raise your arms overhead and intertwine the thumbs so that the palms face forward (see fig. 11.3a). When ready, keep your hips stationary and bend the trunk sideways from one

side to the other as far as possible for three to five repetitions (see figs. 11.3b–c). This exercise stretches mainly the waist.

Hip and Side Stretch

Assume the same position as in the side stretch. In this variant, as you lower the trunk to one side, shift your hips completely to the opposite side. (There is a greater range of motion in this exercise.) Then return to the initial position and bend to the opposite side in the same manner. Repeat two or three times on each side (see figs. 11.4a–b). This exercise gives you a full side stretch, which is needed for full-range weight shift and clearing of the hips to produce a powerful swing and a full follow-through. If you are a long-ball hitter and have a powerful hip slide, do this stretch at least four to six times to fully prepare for such powerful action.

Twisting

Bend over slightly from the hips as in the regular stance, and hold the spine in its neutral curvature. Hold a club in both hands with a pronated grip and with the arms in front of you and perpendicular to the trunk (see fig. 11.5a). Then rotate the shoulders (trunk) to the right and left for four to five repetitions

(a)

Figure 11.2 Lateral arm raise starting position

(b)

Keep the arms straight and raise them out to the sides and overhead.

(a)

Figure 11.3 Side stretch starting position, thumbs intertwined

(b)

Keep your hips stationary.

(c)

Bend the trunk sideways from one side to the other.

(a)

Figure 11.4   As you lower the trunk, shift your hips to the opposite side.

(b)

Return to the initial position and bend to the other side.

(see figs. 11.5b–c). The movement should duplicate the trunk rotation involved in the swing. A variant of this exercise is trunk rotation with a club held behind the back in the crook of both elbows (see figs. 11.6a–c). In this variation, the hips become more involved with the twisting. As a result, the knees will be more active. These twisting exercises also help loosen up the hip joints to get the pelvic girdle ready for action.

Rotator Cuff Stretch

Hold the club in approximately the middle of the shaft in one hand with the arm held in front of you (see fig. 11.7a). Keep the arm straight and rotate the club to the right and to the left (see figs. 11.7b–c). When done, repeat with the other arm for four to six repetitions on each side. This exercise is especially

(a)

Figure 11.5   Twisting starting position

(b)

Rotate the shoulders to the right and left.

(c)

The movement duplicates trunk rotation in the golf swing.

(a)

Figure 11.6 Twisting variation with club in the crook of the arms

(b)

Rotate the shoulders to the right.

(c)

Rotate the shoulders to the left.

(a)

Figure 11.7 Rotator cuff stretch starting position

(b)

Keep the arm straight.

(c)

Rotate the club to the right and to the left. Do both arms.

(a)

Figure 11.8 Protraction and retraction starting position

(b)

Keep the trunk in position and round the shoulders forward.

(c)

Bring the shoulders back as you push your chest forward.

important for the arm rotation that controls clubhead position and allows for a full backswing and follow-through.

Protraction and Retraction

Protraction and retraction help to stretch the shoulders and shoulder girdle in a forward and backward direction. To execute, stand with your arms at your sides (see fig. 11.8a). When ready, keep your trunk in position and move the shoulders as far forward as possible by rounding the shoulders (see fig. 11.8b). Then bring the shoulders back as far to the rear as possible as you push your chest forward (see fig. 11.8c). Repeat three to four times. During execution, only the shoulders should be in motion. This exercise is needed to prevent shoulder injury and to allow a full backswing and follow-through.

Shrug

If you have a tendency toward tightness in the upper shoulders on the sides of the neck, you should do shrugs. With the arms relaxed at your sides, raise

the shoulders (upper traps) as high as possible and hold (see figs. 11.9a–b). After a few seconds, drop them with complete relaxation. Repeat three to four times. When you drop the shoulders quickly, you achieve a greater relaxation effect. This is also a good exercise to do during play if you have a tendency to tighten up.

Good Morning

The good morning is a very important exercise to correctly position the trunk and spine and to actively stretch the hamstrings (see figs. 11.10a–b). Do this exercise three to five times to develop the ability to bend over correctly from the hips not only to position yourself for each shot, but to tee up the ball. It also helps to prevent back problems. Refer to Chapter 4 for a full description of the good morning exercise.

Shoulder Circles

A very important active stretch and warm-up exercise for the shoulders is shoulder circles. Assume a standing position with your arms out so that your body is

(a)

Figure 11.9   Shrug starting position

(b)

Keep the arms relaxed and raise the shoulders as high as possible.

(a)

Figure 11.10   Good morning starting position

(b)

Bend from the hips.

in the shape of the letter *T* (see fig. 11.11a). When ready, begin by rotating the arms up and forward and then down and backward (see figs. 11.11b–c). Make the movement smooth so that the hands circumscribe a circle when viewed from the side. Do not make the circles very large.

After you do five to ten repetitions forward, reverse directions (down and forward and up and backward). You will feel a distinct difference in the muscular involvement between the forward and backward circles. As you do the arm circles, keep the shoulders free. In this way the shoulders will move together with the arms so that both the shoulder girdle and shoulder joint are warmed up, prepared to function at full power.

(a)

Figure 11.11   Shoulder circles starting position

(b)
The hands trace a circle when viewed from the side. Reverse direction after five to ten repetitions.

(c)
Rotate the arms up and forward and then down and backward.

CHAPTER

12

Golf and Nutrition

Role of Nutrition

Nutrition and diets are some of the most sensationalized topics in the press. It is difficult to pick up a magazine or newspaper or listen to a news report without another "amazing" or "startling" discovery in this field. For example, broccoli, the miracle food; oat bran, the miracle product to lower cholesterol; the high-carbohydrate, low-fat diet to lose weight; or the eat-all-you-want-and-lose-weight-fast diet. Suffice it to say that the truth and substantiation of the statements has been skewed to the extreme.

The bottom line is that if you want to play a great game of golf, you are going to have to give your body the right fuels. Hunger pangs, headaches, bizarre supplements, cravings, fasts, and binges, all typical outcomes of being on a diet or not eating well, will not help you do this. If you do more playing or exercising, you will only end up grumpy, tired, discouraged, and depressed. Rather than looking at the diet, you blame the exercise program or your golf game for how badly you feel. Please don't make this mistake.

Your diet must satisfy your mouth as well as your muscles, and there must be a way of eating that you can live with over the long haul. The only "diet" you should be on is the one you can stay on and enjoy for life. In essence, your eating habits must be part of your lifestyle.

Developing Optimal Nutrition

Playing golf without the right diet is like trying to run your car without sufficient fuel or oil. Sooner or later the car is going to break down or, at best, just plain run out of gas. Think of food not as an enemy, but rather as an ally—and a very important one. Why? Because of a simple phenomenon known as *supercompensation*. It occurs in response to what is known as a *training effect*.

For example, if you go on an exercise program and play more golf than you are used to, your body will experience a greater workload than it is accustomed to. As a result, you deplete the body's energy supplies in order to get the work accomplished. After the work is done, recovery begins to take place and some of the energy stores are replaced so that you have enough energy to continue doing various tasks during the day.

The real recovery, however, takes place when you are sleeping. It is at this time that the body goes to work not only to repair any damage that was done to the muscles, but also to restructure the muscles and support structures in response to the exercises or playing done. The glycogen stores are replenished, which brings the energy levels back up, and other various functions return your body to a stable state.

However, the body does not just compensate for what you have done or merely replace the energy supply that it originally had. Because the body does not like to be stressed, it deposits additional energy stores so that the next time you do this amount of work, the body will have an ample reserve, which, in turn, allows you to do even more. This is what is known as supercompensation. If you do not do sufficient work, your body will never get to the point of bringing about supercompensation, and you will merely be recovering or simply replacing what was used up.

You probably experienced supercompensation when you first began to play. After your first round of eighteen you were probably quite tired, especially if you walked the course. However, as you kept playing and walking the course, you eventually were able to play without undue fatigue. Thus, in the very early stages of playing, your body overcompensated. But once you were accustomed to the playing, your body merely replaced the energy supply that was used up, and you once again returned to your normal state.

If you want to improve your capabilities, you have to exert yourself physically to get a training effect. You need supercompensation for additional strength, flexibility, endurance, and other physical qualities. Supercompensation is your ticket to making progress not only in your golf game, but in your physical development. But to make the needed changes, your body must have the necessary nutrients at its disposal. If you are lacking the nutrients needed, the changes will not take place to improve your abilities!

For your golf game and exercise program to be most successful, you must have the fuels to make the body changes you need. Eating well is not difficult and does not require extensive recordkeeping. The key is not to count the calories but to choose a wide variety of the right kinds of foods in the right amounts, and eat at opportune times.

Elements of Nutrition

Fats

Dietary fat has been on just about everyone's nutritional chopping block, with some legitimate reasons. Fat is calorically denser than protein or carbohydrates. A single gram contains nine calories, while a gram of protein or carbohydrate contains only about four. But there are good fats and bad fats. Only diets high in saturated fat and trans-fats (hydrogenated oils) appear to be a risk factor for obesity, heart disease, high blood pressure, stroke, diabetes, and even some forms of cancer.

A high-fat diet typically leaves you feeling sluggish, so that you will not be able to play or exercise at your best. Also, dietary fat has a pronounced tendency to become body fat, once consumed. That is especially true of saturated fat, the kind found in fatty meats, full-fat dairy products, palm and coconut oil, and, yes, even margarine, which contains trans-fats.

Fat must never be eliminated from the diet. You should only reduce drastically the amount of saturated fat you take in, but eat ample amounts of mono- and polyunsaturated fats. The body needs fat for many functions, which include assimilating fat-soluble vitamins and manufacturing cell walls and certain essential enzymes and hormones. Fat also helps make food both more satisfying and more filling.

Limit your intake of dietary fat to no more than 25 to 30 percent of your daily caloric intake. Start simply by cutting down on the most obvious foods, such as fried foods, rich sauces, hamburgers, hot dogs, full-fat salad dressings, mayonnaise, and rich desserts. Use good oils, such as olive, canola, peanut, safflower, flaxseed, walnut, and fish.

An excellent way to get good fats is to eat raw nuts as a snack. Use butter instead of margarine. Even though the virtues of margarine have been extolled for many years, we now know that it has many more negative effects than does butter. Butter is a natural product that the body can assimilate, while margarine (a trans-fatty acid) acts the same as a saturated fat and remains in your body for extended periods of time. Eat plenty of fish and fish oils, especially if you have a tendency to overdo the saturated fats, to help move the saturated fats out of the body.

Proteins

Proteins (amino acids) are very important, as they provide the basic building blocks for cellular muscular repair and development and provide energy. While carbohydrates and fats supply most of the energy for muscular exertion, protein enables your muscles to respond to this exertion by getting firmer and stronger. This is why your need for protein increases the more you put your muscles to work. Exercise causes the muscles to undergo a type of intricate cellular breakdown that only protein can repair and build upon.

Playing golf and being on a regular exercise program means that you should be getting approximately one half to one gram of protein daily for every pound you weigh. The exact amount will depend upon your age, intensity and duration of the workouts, and your level of development. Some of the best sources of protein are lean meats, poultry, fish, dairy products, whole-grain cereals and breads, beans, and nuts.

Carbohydrates

Carbohydrates are great for fast energy, and in some ways are the most healthful type of food you can eat. This includes such foods as pasta, cereals, breads, potatoes, rice, beans, fruits, and vegetables. Carbohydrates should be eaten in their natural, "complex" forms. Potato chips and candy bars don't count!

The more energy you have, the more likely you will have high-quality golf games and workouts. Some carbohydrates are unique; they "rev-up" your body's metabolic rate, even when you're just resting,

and once you begin to exercise, carbohydrates really begin to kick into gear. But they are of relatively short duration. When you play 18 holes, fats become most important about halfway through.

Fiber

Fiber keeps your digestive system in shape and affects the shape of your body because of its role in excretion of dietary fat. Get enough fiber in your diet and you help "sweep" dietary fat through your intestines before it has a chance to be fully absorbed. This spares not only your waistline, but also your arteries and heart. Note that the best sources of fiber are foods rich in high-energy carbohydrates (grains, potatoes, beans). Try to get approximately 30 grams of fiber a day, which is roughly twice the amount the average American routinely consumes.

Helpful Eating Hints

You don't have to look far to find the kinds of foods that will enable you to function at your best. For example: grains are nutrient storehouses, rich in vitamins and minerals, and provide great amounts of energy. No wonder that grains, along with beans, serve as a staple for so many cultures.

To fulfill your quota of these valuable complex carbohydrates, think beyond the popular white rice and white flour baked goods. Choose from whole-grain products and go for variety. Cornbread, muffins, and pancakes made with whole grains and little fat are fine, but avoid fat-enhanced baking goods such as biscuits and high-fat quick breads. And stay away from corn chips, donuts, potato chips, high-fat crackers, cookies, cakes, and sweet rolls.

Vegetables are another mainstay of your diet. When you make a salad, instead of using iceberg lettuce, which has little nutritional value, use dark leaf lettuce such as romaine and red leaf. In addition to lettuce, different kinds of greens, such as spinach, can be included. Add items such as celery, green peppers, red onions, red cabbage, broccoli, cauliflower, carrots, or any raw vegetable you enjoy. To further liven up salads, work in some foods from the grains and legumes group.

In this way, you can consume hundreds of satisfying calories, while taking in minimum amounts of fat. Also, keep a couple of sealed plastic bags of raw cut-up veggies handy in your crisper. Broccoli, carrots, zucchini, cauliflower, asparagus, green or red peppers, pea pods, fresh green beans, chick-peas, mushrooms, turnips, and tomatoes are great for snacks during the day and on the golf course.

Fresh fruit quenches your thirst and fills you up. Whole or pureed fruit is a reliable source of fiber. Go for the whole fruit, preferably locally grown and naturally ripened, since it is more satisfying and nutritious. Fruit in season is more likely to be fresh.

Yogurt and cheese are also important in your diet, along with meat, poultry, fish, beans, eggs, and nuts. As discussed earlier, protein is very important, but eat mostly lean meats to get your full complement of amino acids and less saturated fat. Concentrate on foods rich in high-quality protein, such as lean meats, poultry, beans, and fish. Fresh raw nuts and seeds are an excellent source of protein, fiber, vitamins, and minerals.

Eggs are not the culprits in increasing your cholesterol levels—the real culprit is the feed that chickens eat! The feed is devoid of many products such as lecithin, the key to breaking up cholesterol and moving it through the body. In other words, the adulterated chicken food that is lacking in nutrients makes the eggs major sources of cholesterol! Natural eggs will not give you higher levels of cholesterol. These eggs can be found in most stores under the label of "cage-free," "fertile," or "range-free" eggs.

Fat-Free Foods

The number of fat-free foods has increased astronomically over the past few years, as have low-fat substitutes. However, studies are showing that people now eat more fat than they did before, and are still gaining weight and becoming heavier because they are eating more. Thus, the culprit is not simply eating food with fat. It is best to eat food with the fat in its natural state and to eat it sparingly. But a

major problem is finding many products in their natural state!

A serious drawback to eating low-fat and no-fat foods is that the reconstituted versions of the real thing lack fat-soluble nutrients and possibly other undiscovered nutrients. Scientists are still discovering new vitamins and minerals that up until now were not thought to be important to human health! To be sure you are getting an adequate supply of everything you need, your diet should include foods that are as close as possible to their natural state, and that includes fat.

Don't rely too heavily on artificial sweeteners. Again, studies have found that over the course of a year, people who use artificial sweeteners are more likely to gain weight than nonusers because the artificial sweeteners may increase feelings of hunger. One of the reasons for this is that the brain interprets all sweeteners equally and triggers changes in blood sugar that mimic a reaction to sugar.

Differences Between Men and Women

According to one of the top clinical nutritionists, Dr. Tobin Watkinson, it appears that women do not react the same way to some carbohydrates as men. He has found that women can actually gain weight when they eat carbohydrates such as pastas, breads, and potatoes. Most men, however, do not react this way. This may explain why some people, especially women, often get sleepy after eating certain carbohydrates. The carbohydrates seem to react in the body the same way protein does in others. Some men appear to react the same way. Because of this, you should pay close attention to how you react to certain foods and eat accordingly. We are all unique individuals!

Keep It Simple

When it comes to preparing food, less is better. Don't overcook vegetables or obliterate otherwise healthy foods with high-fat cooking techniques such as deep-frying or sautéing in gobs of lard or butter. It has been my experience that foods eaten as close as possible to their natural state provide maximum taste and nutrition with minimum fuss. So do yourself a favor: leave the time-consuming and calorie-added gourmet cooking techniques to French chefs. Try to appreciate foods for what they are as opposed to what they become once adulterated by some high-fat garnish or sauce, and you will be ahead of the game.

Think Mini-Meals

If you are most active in the morning or early day, and like to retire early, your evening meal should be relatively light, while breakfast or lunch should be "heavy." Eat at least three times a day and have a mini-snack midmorning and midafternoon. No meal skipping, and especially no fasting allowed. Your body is a finely tuned machine that needs fuel (nutrition) on a regular basis. Skipping meals is counterproductive to weight control because it slows down fat burning by slowing down the metabolism. Worse yet, it sets up the likelihood of another classic eating blunder: the binge, which treats fat cells to a smorgasbord.

The next time you are feeling too busy to eat and don't have time for a conventional meal, there is nothing wrong with a healthful snack, such as fruits, nuts, or a container of yogurt. There are even some natural food products such as the Standardbar by Standard Process. This product is made out of whole, natural foods and serves as an energetic protein-type food that also helps you to recover after workouts. People who are successful in maintaining a normal weight find that in addition to exercising regularly, they eat as many as five or six mini-meals a day.

Drink Lots of Water

Water, ample amounts of water, is extremely important to a golfer, because it not only keeps you hydrated enough to play with maximum efficiency, but it also helps your body cool itself and get rid of its natural waste products. When you exercise you lose water, not just through sweat but also through your breathing, and the losses can be substantial.

This doesn't mean that sweating is negative—it is natural and desirable. Perspiration cools the body, gets rid of waste products, and cleanses the pores. But it does deplete the body of water that must be replaced, so play it safe. Drink at least eight to nine eight-ounce glasses of water a day, which does not include soda, coffee, or tea. And don't wait till you're thirsty to drink. Your body can be short of water without your thirst letting you know about it.

Keep Hydrated

According to Dr. Watkinson, the only thing that can totally rehydrate the cells is water. You can survive on colas, soft drinks, iced tea, or sparkling mineral waters, but they will not rehydrate the cell the way water will. Water is the universal solvent. It enters the cell, rehydrates it, and carries the waste materials away. You will not get these results with other drinks. The reason for this is that the pH in most drinks is inappropriate for the body. A carbonated drink is very acidic, versus being alkaline, which would better rehydrate the cell.

There are now a lot of designer waters around, and many are touted as rehydration drinks. The unfortunate thing about these drinks is that they only contain one or two electrolytes and their major ingredient is some form of sugar. It may taste good at the moment, but you will not be feeling very well twenty minutes to an hour later. At this time you may need more, or you will lose your concentration.

Thus, it's best to have water-containing minerals such as calcium, magnesium, potassium, and sodium. Some drinking waters have these elements—for example, microwater. This water not only rehydrates the body more easily, but it is a very powerful antioxidant, which takes care of the free radicals that are formed during play and work. Another good water is one that has been oxygenated. Oxy-Water, for example, contains extra oxygen, which is beneficial to recovery. It may help you when playing in hot weather, especially during the latter nine holes.

Rehydration is very important to a golfer, and you should drink two or more liters of water a day, depending upon your activity level. Keep in mind that you are about 80 percent water yourself, and you need to have a continuous supply of good water. Today, most of our water is basically a chemical bath—it is no longer "natural" water.

Food Versus Pills

I cannot overemphasize the importance of eating fresh and natural foods whenever possible. Don't let yourself be duped by the fantastic advertising claims often made for certain high-price health foods and supplements. If you eat wisely and eat a variety of pesticide-free foods from the different categories, you shouldn't need many additional supplements. Supplementation, as the term implies, is to *supplement* your diet.

If you find your diet lacking, or your food sources are grown in land that is depleted in nutrients, or where the plants are fed mainly synthetic (chemical) fertilizers, or if there are environmental conditions that lower the value of foods, then supplementation becomes very important. For example, because so much food is now grown chemically as opposed to organically, where vegetation, foodstuffs, and manures are put back into the soil to keep it rich in nutrients, supplementation is often required. The reason for this is that chemically grown food will never have the full spectrum of nutrients that occur in nature. To understand this, it is important to know the differences between what constitutes natural as opposed to synthetic supplements or food.

Synthetic Versus Natural

In the nutritional literature, the term *natural* is often used synonymously with *synthetic*. In reality, however, they are worlds apart. Thus, it is important to understand what a truly natural supplement is as opposed to one that is called "natural" but in reality is synthetic. For example, in nature a vitamin is not a single ingredient—it is a complex entitiy, composed of many different factors. This includes organic nutrients, enzymes, co-enzymes, antioxidants, and trace minerals. Enzymes are proteins and contain amino acids and trace minerals.

According to Dr. Royal Lee, every mineral needed by the living cell is commonly found in a natural assemblage of vitamin concentrates. Clinical nutritionist Judith DeCava supports this position in her statements that enzyme activators may include trace elements such as manganese, cobalt, zinc,

copper, molybdenum, selenium, vanadium, and so on. These components are effective only when in the proper organic, organized state. In other words, a vitamin, more accurately a vitamin complex, contains many different ingredients, factors that are indigenous to the food that make up the vitamin's organic unity and entirety.

There are even changes in organic makeup with the seasons. Some food products that mature in the spring have a different vitamin complex than do products that mature in the summertime. This is why it is important to eat foods that are in season so that you get a full complement of the various vitamins, minerals, and other organic nutrients as they basically occur in nature.

It is commonly believed that there is little difference between organically grown foods and commercially grown foods. However, some recent research disputes this in a very dramatic way. For example, a study done at Rutgers University found major differences between commercially and organically grown foods. In the study, commercial foods such as spinach, tomatoes, and lettuce were compared to the same foods grown organically.

In regard to iron in tomatoes, there were 1,938 parts per million in organically grown tomatoes and only 1 part per million in commercially grown tomatoes. Organically grown tomatoes had 53 and 0.63 part per million, respectively, of copper and cobalt, while the commercial counterparts had 0. Spinach showed similar results. Organic spinach had 1,584 parts per million of iron, while the commercial source had only 49. In regard to manganese, copper, and cobalt, the organic spinach scored 117, 32, and 0.25, respectively, while the commercial counterparts were 1, 0.3, and 0.2, respectively. These are not minor differences. They are highly significant and show how the commercially grown foods are lacking in many essential nutrients.

According to DeCava, because of the need for objectivity in scientific research, legitimate research on vitamins becomes impossible when using the total natural complex. In science, it is necessary to isolate only one of the ingredients in order to check on its effects without consideration of the other factors with which it is naturally associated in nature. As a result, when the synthetic or "pure" forms of the vitamins are developed, they duplicate only a fraction of the vitamin as it appears in nature. In essence, the vitamin becomes a crystalline pure chemical that hardly resembles the original intricate vitamin complex.

Because vitamin complexes are so intricate, it is almost impossible to artificially duplicate the entire complex as it occurs in its organic natural state. To my knowledge, all attempts to do this have been unsuccessful. For example, the crystalline or chemically pure vitamin, when separated from its other components, has its biological activity destroyed. In addition, since it does not contain the trace mineral activators, it cannot function as a biochemical catalyst.

Perhaps even more important, when you take the chemically pure vitamins that are lacking the other ingredients with which they are naturally associated, it may create a vitamin deficiency in the body. According to Dr. Tobin Watkinson, it is generally assumed that ascorbic acid is vitamin C. However, ascorbic acid is only one component of vitamin C. Think of ascorbic acid as the shell of the egg. The yolk and white parts contain the enzymes, mineral activators, and trace minerals that make up the entire complex of the vitamin.

When you take only ascorbic acid, it seeks out the other components that make up the vitamin complex after it enters the body. As a result, it robs the body of these nutrients in order to complete itself and to function as a true vitamin. If enough of the synthetic vitamin is taken in, it may rob the body of the other essential components to such an extent that the body becomes deficient in other vitamins! It is a paradoxical situation since the more you use the synthetic vitamin, the more you may be depriving yourself of that particular vitamin. As a result, you may be creating other problems in the body that rely on particular vitamins for proper functioning.

Many studies that have been conducted with vitamins show different results when the natural complex is used as opposed to the synthetic form. In most cases, the natural complex was found to be effective in preventing many diseases, while the synthetic not only did not prevent various diseases, but actually contributed to some! Thus, a synthetic vitamin can only be used for a drug effect since it can mask symptoms but does not alleviate the cause of the illness, disease, or injury.

For example, in a seven-year study of male Finnish smokers supplemented with synthetic betacarotene and/or synthetic vitamin E, it was found that the groups taking the betacarotene actually experienced a greater increase in lung cancer. Those taking synthetic vitamin E had a greater incidence of stroke and heart attacks. The control group, which was not fortified with the synthetic vitamins, showed hardly any change! If the natural forms of vitamin A and vitamin E were used, the results may have been substantially different.

According to DeCava, it is important to recognize that living things can only be reproduced from living things. Chemically pure refined synthetic vitamins are made from dead, inert materials. Natural foods contain live vitamins, organic minerals, enzymes, and other vital functional live components, all organized by the sun, rain, water, soils, nutrients, and living bacteria. When live natural foods are denatured (made dead), their individual vitamin parts may be chemically identical to the synthetic, but not so when in a live state.

A similar problem occurs in chemical farming. The soil becomes more and more depleted and the plant becomes less nutritious. As a result, when we eat the final product, we do not derive the essential ingredients that the plant is supposed to have, as, for example, when grown organically (with natural products being put back into the soil).

In addition, because of the way many of our natural foods are being treated, it is sometimes difficult to tell if they are alive or dead. For example, look closely at the potatoes you buy. Do you see any "eyes" in the potato? If you do not, it is probably because the potato has been irradiated (exposed to radioactive material) to kill all bugs that may attack it so that the potato has a longer shelf life. However, without the eyes from which the new growth takes place when the potato reproduces, new potatoes will not grow from the irradiated potato. Thus, aside from the radiation that you are accumulating and the negative effects that you are experiencing from eating nutritionally deficient foods, are you now eating a live potato or one that is already dead?

Because of the difficulty in eating truly natural foods as they occur in nature, it is important to often supplement for some of the needed missing ingredients. One way to find out what you are lacking is to have various tests done to check for possible deficiencies. There are tests available today that indicate the need for certain nutrients—for example, a symptom survey of how you feel and react. There are also various blood tests that can be used.

However, when using supplements, be sure that the supplement is made from whole foods and not from chemicals. For example, the supplements by Standard Process, which I have been using for many years, are made from whole, organically grown foods. They make a wide variety of different products that cover a full spectrum of needs.

These nutrients or supplements cannot be purchased over-the-counter and are sold only to physicians and professionals who in turn prescribe them to their patients. This helps ensure that you do not overdose on particular vitamins, and that you take them when the body actually calls for them. Taking additional supplements, especially the synthetic varieties, when the body does not need them can be as dangerous as not having a sufficient amount. Do not think that excesses are simply washed out of the system. For more information on Standard Process, call (800) 848-5061 or write to Standard Process, 1200 West Royal Lee Drive, Palmyra, WI 53156.

Enjoy Your Food

With a little imagination and not a lot of work, you can make your healthy diet extremely enjoyable. If your diet isn't giving you pleasure, it is lacking in some aspects, regardless of how nutritionally complete it may be. Important, too, is allowing yourself some of your favorite foods, because cravings tell you something about your body's chemistry. A craving for something sweet, for example, could be a sign that your blood sugar has fallen too low. (Don't make this a habit, though.) Or a strong urge for something salty could mean that the sweat that you are losing in your workouts or playing has caused your body's sodium levels to dip. Use pure sea salt for replenishment, not processed salt, which can be detrimental.

Learn to respect your body's messages, because they are usually telling you something you should know. When you do partake in something a little special, don't feel guilty about it. Erase guilt from your vocabulary. If you are exercising regularly, the food will have a purpose. In fact, the more you play and exercise, the more you will automatically find yourself migrating to better and healthier foods, mainly because you will see the difference in your abilities and how you feel.

Many healthy and beneficial foods are also very tasty. For example, the product that I typically recommend for a snack is the Standardbar by Standard Process. This product is made out of natural whole foods and has a multitude of different vitamins, minerals, and other foodstuffs. It is great not only as a snack, but also as a meal replacement or when you do not have time to eat a regular full meal. Many professional golfers eat the Standardbar during play.

Special Considerations
Emotions

Your emotions can also play a major role in the number of calories you burn and the amount of energy you possess. This is especially important for golfers, since golf is often a very emotional game. Studies show that athletes can burn up to 25 percent more energy in competition than they do in practice. This is a considerable amount of energy. It also explains why many people who seem to be on the go all the time appear to use up a tremendous amount of nervous energy, which, in turn, burns a great number of calories. Because of this, it is important to take the emotions into consideration not only when playing golf, but also in various work and family situations.

Specific Nutritional Needs

For more golf-specific nutritional information, I interviewed Dr. Tobin Watkinson, one of the leading clinical nutritionists, who has worked with golfers and other athletes. He stated that energy expenditure in the golf game depends to a good extent on whether you are playing in the morning or afternoon, and on the emotional factors involved.

According to Dr. Watkinson, as you start off your game, your energy levels are usually high. But as you start moving through your game, your body begins to burn different fuels. Initially you use a fair amount of the sugars (carbohydrates) that are present in your body from the stores of glycogen. Once you have depleted the sugars, your body goes to burning fats. Thus, most golfers probably burn sugar for the first nine holes, and more fats for the last nine. Because of this, you may see a difference in your game between the first and second nine holes. Some golfers actually feel the shift that occurs as the fuels change.

Your brain runs on one fuel and one fuel only: sugar. If you can't get sugar from your liver, the body will go to the adrenals, at which time you may find yourself getting angry, irritated, or frustrated. Anyone who has ever played golf can identify with these feelings that occur when there is inadequate conversion of stored sugars (the usable sugars), forcing the body to go to the adrenals for more energy.

In addition, if you have inadequate sugars, your liver can convert certain amino acids (serine, glycine, and alanine) for energy. These amino acids are converted into sugar in the liver, which can then be used to run your brain. To help encourage this process make sure that you have an ample amount of protein in your diet. This is a major part of the golf game!

The Morning Golfer

If you play in the morning and didn't eat breakfast or ate an inadequate breakfast, you will find that you will run out of energy much more quickly than your opponents. This is especially true if they had an appropriate breakfast—at least for the first nine. On the back nine, when you are out of sugar and your body looks to fats to burn, you shunt your brain, cutting off its nutritional needs. Thus your concentration is down and your frustration levels may mount greatly.

Consequently, you should time your meals so that if you are a morning person, you have your heavier starch, protein, and vegetables for breakfast. An omelet would be an excellent food to have. The midmorning snack should include nuts and seeds for proteins, which keep your sugars up but don't give you an overabundance. They will run your brain very well. It is best to have nuts raw and unsalted unless you are playing in some very hot weather, at which time a little salt is good.

It is best to have nuts and seeds alone since they can be digested easily and more efficiently on an empty stomach. Understand that when nuts and seeds get cooked with salt and oil, they go bad easily and may cause headaches and other problems.

If you are an afternoon or evening person and must play a morning golf game, you should start your day with fruit and then have a midmorning snack of some substantial protein, such as beef jerky. Evening persons need to have the fruits in the morning to raise their blood sugar. If you have some fruit and then a vegetable snack while out playing, you will do better.

These recommendations are for golfers who are serious about their golf game. When you have an energy problem (when your first nine holes look a lot better than your back nine, or your first nine look terrible and your back nine look fine), then you have to start looking at what you are taking onto the golf course with you.

The Afternoon Golfer

For an afternoon golf game, lunch is the same for a morning person and for an afternoon person. Do not limit your lunch to pasta or a sandwich. A morning person should have starch in the morning, and a night person should have starch at night. In regard to protein, if you have too much at lunch, you'll get tired in the afternoon and you'll find yourself yawning in the middle of the game. Thus, too much starch or too much protein will be converted to sugars, making them inappropriate for lunch. An appropriate lunch would be lots of above-ground vegetables, and a little protein, such as fish or chicken.

Drinking soft drinks or alcohol can be detrimental. The alcohol will dehydrate you and will affect your blood sugar, as will soft drinks. Any of the sugary soft drinks and fruit juices that you would think would be great are, in fact, not very nutritious. For example, how many real oranges does it take to make a glass of orange juice? Not many people would sit down and eat the four or five oranges that it takes to make a glass of orange juice. If you must have juice, then you should water it down. Eating the whole fruit is much better than just having the juice.

If you are a morning person in the middle of an afternoon golf game, you need to have a snack of some fruit. If you are a night person, you should have the nuts in the middle of an afternoon game that the morning person had in the middle of their morning. Keep in mind that you need the protein to make it through to your dinner.

Concentration

Golfers need to maintain their concentration throughout the game, and especially near the end of the game. Concentration is basically brain chemistry, a balance between your ability to utilize the fuel that you have taken in and your ability to convert it into the appropriate brain chemistries. All the amino acids, which are the small building blocks of proteins, are the precursors to building the brain chemistries we hear much about today. This includes serotonin, melatonin, epinephrine, and norepinephrine, as well as the other products that our brains need to be able to function as needed.

If you are out playing and are under stress, you are going to use a higher amount of your brain fuels. If you are unable to replenish these fuels due to the burning up of the raw material or not having adequate raw material, your body will "stall out." If you have a high demand, as, for example, when you are in a golf tournament or you are playing several rounds, and your body does not have the appropriate fuels to do what is needed, then you will be unable to concentrate.

To prevent this, be sure to have a wide range of foods and to follow the guidelines presented above. This means having vegetables, proteins, nuts, seeds, and some fruit in order to get a full range of these very rich sources of all the vitamins and minerals. Unfortunately, many people today are taking synthetic and incomplete vitamins that actually create vitamin deficiencies. We cannot produce a nutrient that is as complete as what nature can produce.

13

The Exercise Program

Basic Development

Designing Your Exercise Program

For your exercise program to be most effective, you must individualize it according to your swing and physical abilities. For example, the amount of resistance that you use, the kind and number of exercises that you execute, and the number of sets and reps used for each exercise depend on your mastery of the exercises and your mastery of the golf swing.

As you read the following material, select what applies to you. However, keep in mind that as your level of fitness and mastery of the exercises improves, you should move up to the next level of difficulty.

Level 1: Beginner

Level 1 is a learning and familiarization stage. It is used to accustom your body gradually to exercise without soreness or discomfort. To begin, read (and sometimes reread) exactly how to do the exercises. Have this book with you when you work out. Since all of the exercises can be done at home, you can do them at your leisure and with privacy.

Getting Started

Do one exercise for three to five repetitions with light resistance. When using Active Cords, adjust the length so that you can execute the exercise easily through a full range of motion. This means that you do the exercise (up and down or away and back) three to four times. Execute each repetition at a moderate rate of speed.

As you do the exercise, concentrate on exactly how you are doing it and how it feels to your body. In this way you will recognize what each exercise feels like and which muscles are working. After completing three to five repetitions, relax and then get ready for the next exercise. Read the description and then do several repetitions. Proceed in this manner until you do all the exercises selected.

You do not have to do every exercise that is described in this book for each phase of the swing. Pick out exercises for your troublesome areas or swing actions you would like to improve. Other exercises can be attempted the following week, or as you get used to doing the core (for you) exercises. For example, a sample exercise program may include the following exercises:

- Good morning
- Back raise
- Leg abduction
- Reverse trunk twist
- Forward hip rotation
- Medial and lateral shoulder rotation
- Ulnar and radial flexion

If you desire more improvement of particular actions or phases of the swing, include more exercises. However, for most golfers this sample program is quite sufficient for the first two to four weeks, especially in regard to learning the exercises. It is important that you record each exercise and the number of repetitions that you do. To help you in this endeavor, a sample record sheet can be found on page 123. A record keeping book is also available.

Reps and Sets

Keep adding one or two repetitions at each workout (or each week) until you reach fifteen to twenty repetitions maximum (RM—the most you can do without undue stress). You will reach fifteen to twenty RM fairly rapidly in some exercises, while in other exercises progress may be much slower. This is perfectly normal, since some muscles take longer to respond and certain exercises are easier to learn than others. When you repeatedly reach twenty (or more) RM you will be ready to work out on Level 2 for that particular exercise.

If you experience soreness on or after any workout day, you did too many repetitions or used too much resistance! In this case, you should not increase the repetitions or resistance on the following workout day. Instead, use the same weight or even less resistance to help your body recover. When you feel ready, then you can gradually increase the resistance or the repetitions.

After a few weeks, you will become more comfortable with the exercises and have greater confidence. Since you will be able to handle more resistance and execute more repetitions without any discomfort or

trepidation, you may want to add other exercises at this time.

Workout Frequency

You should work out a minimum of three days per week. The workouts should not last more than a maximum of twenty to thirty minutes at this time. That's right, twenty to thirty minutes! This is not a long time. Thus, for a maximum of ninety minutes a week, you can gain the strength and flexibility that will enable you to achieve a more effective swing and to play on a higher level more quickly.

Each of you is a unique individual who will respond to exercises differently. This is why you should never copy what someone else is doing. Because someone you know may have responded quickly to these exercises, it does not mean that your body will also respond in the same manner. This is especially true in the senior years.

If you copy someone else's program, regardless of how successful it is, you take a chance of getting injured. Not only may the resistance be greater than what your muscles and joints can handle, but the way the exercise is executed by another person may not fit the way your body is designed to move. In these instances, there is a high likelihood of injury. Your program must be individualized, just as your golf swing is very individual.

It is important that you work out on a regular basis. When on a three-days-per-week program, you must not skip days and say, "I will do four days next week because I only did two this week." This is not effective. Working out more than three days per week does not bring additional benefits, but it can lead to overtraining and the possibility of injury and soreness. A three-day-a-week program allows for a day's rest in-between to give your muscles ample time to fully recover. As a result, it will not interfere with your golf playing!

Keep Swinging

To get maximum benefit from the strength and flexibility exercise program, you should continue playing (or hitting practice balls) to constantly make

Sample Record Sheet

Date: _____   **Time:** _____

Exercise Goal: _____

Exercise	Set 1 Number of reps	Resistance cord color or weight	Set 2 Number of reps	Resistance cord color or weight	Set 3 Number of reps	Resistance cord color or weight	Set 4 Number of reps	Resistance cord color or weight
1								
2								
3								
4								
5								
6								
7								
8								
9								
10								
11								
12								
13								
14								
15								
16								
17								
18								
19								
20								

Feeling during/after exercise: _____

Other information: _____

what should now be natural adjustments in your swing. Most of them will be made unconsciously because of the muscular feel developed when doing the exercises. The swing changes will feel so natural that you will hardly notice them.

Schedule your workouts so that they are not done immediately before your playing or practicing. An ideal situation would be to do the exercises in the morning and to play golf in the afternoon. If you prefer playing golf in the morning, then you should do the exercises in late afternoon or evening. The key here is to give yourself a few hours of rest and recovery in-between. Do the exercises consistently and at a fairly regular time so that you have a full twenty-four to forty-eight hours for recovery and so that your body may adapt to the exercises.

Level 2: Intermediate

On Level 2, when you reach about twenty RM, regularly increase the resistance. Doing this increases the intensity and should bring you down to twelve to fifteen RM. Then work back up to twenty RM and repeat the process. When you do an exercise for fifteen to twenty RM, it is important that the last repetitions be the most that you can do with proper technique. Do not, for example, do fifteen to twenty repetitions and still feel refreshed. When you finish the set, you should feel slightly out of breath and have muscular fatigue.

Be in tune with your body as you do the exercises. Only in this way can you find out what is working for you and determine which exercises appear to be most effective. You can then make the necessary changes in the exercises or exercise program to produce the results that you desire. If you feel you need more work on certain muscles, add another set of selected exercises.

You can change your body (within your genetic limits) or golf swing a great deal, depending not only on which exercises you use, but also how many repetitions and sets you use. A set means doing a particular number of repetitions of one exercise one time. For example, if you did twenty repetitions of the reverse trunk twist, this constitutes one set. After

a short rest of one to two minutes, you again do twenty repetitions of the same exercise. This is then considered the second set.

Level 3: Advanced

On Level 3, you should be ready to do two to three sets of the key exercises. This increased number of sets is used to gain greater strength and endurance. Using greater resistance, which is needed for strength, requires warm-up or preparation of the muscles. Thus, for the first set (when doing three sets), do ten repetitions with half the resistance that you will be using in the second set. In the second set, do eight to ten RM. Follow this with the third set in which you do fifteen to twenty RM.

After you do the first set, rest for approximately thirty to sixty seconds, and then repeat for the second set. If desired, you can do another exercise for different muscles between sets. In this way, you do not have to wait for a particular muscle to recover, and as a result, you can do more exercises in a shorter amount of time.

Completing three sets—a set for warm-up, a set for strength, and a set for endurance—should be sufficient for most golfers. However, I have known some golfers who like to execute four sets of selected exercises or do many exercises per session. This is fine as long as you go through a full range of motion in each exercise and balance the muscular development with other exercises. There is no need for very great resistance in this program. If you use too much resistance, your range of motion will decrease, which, in turn, can negatively affect your swing. Thus, be sure that you do the exercises exactly as described, regardless of how many sets or exercises you do.

Overview: Exercise Levels

Level 1: Start with three to four reps of each exercise, mainly for learning and confidence building. Work out three times per week with gradual increases in repetitions up to fifteen to twenty RM.

Level 2: Do fifteen to twenty RM of each exercise three times per week. You should now have confidence in doing the exercises and be capable of pushing your body to accomplish the work. Increase the resistance when reaching twenty RM and repeat the buildup.

Level 3: At this time you should be capable of doing two to three sets of selected exercises with greater intensity.

Helpful Hints

In the early stages of training, complete only one set of fifteen to twenty RM. This is needed to develop greater circulatory system capillaries, which enables the muscles to recover faster so that you can play and exercise more frequently. High repetitions in the early stages of training strengthen the ligaments and tendons. This does not occur to the same extent when doing only a few repetitions with greater resistance. The high-repetition routine also results in greater strength and muscular endurance in the initial stages, both of which are needed for golf as well as for your daily activities.

When doing a fifteen to twenty RM set, you develop mainly muscular endurance, together with increased blood flow in the early repetitions of a set. However, as you reach the last five to six repetitions in the set, the stress on the muscles becomes the same as though you were using heavy resistance for only a few repetitions, the key to greater strength.

To ensure these gains, you should experience some "straining" as you complete the last few repetitions, but it should be within your capabilities. Placing such stress on the body is needed for true physiological changes to occur. This includes restructuring of the muscles and tissues, which allows you to do more work and to experience positive body changes.

I must strongly emphasize the need to push yourself after you are accustomed to the exercises and exercise program. Many individuals have failed in their previous programs because they did not push to the point of attaining the greatest value from the exercises. Build up gradually so that when you are doing fifteen to twenty RM, your body will be accustomed to the stress and you will see positive changes occurring not only physically but mentally.

Doing more than one set when first beginning usually leads to overstress and soreness, and may interfere with your game. In addition, it may cause injury or illness.

When you are accustomed to the exercises and have more energy, you can do more sets per exercise. This typically applies to a more fit golfer. Thus, the exact number of sets and repetitions that you use must be individually determined to meet your abilities and desires.

Mastering the beginning- and intermediate-level workouts will be more than sufficient for most golfers to effectively improve their swing and game. However, if you desire even greater levels of strength and endurance, you should exercise on Level 3 to experience even more benefits.

The more slowly you gain strength over a long period of time, the longer it will be with you when you do not work out. The more quickly you gain strength, the more quickly you will lose it if you do not continue the workouts. And you do not have to continually increase the resistance or the number of repetitions or sets. When you reach a level that enables you to play the game the way you like, then all you have to do is maintain your strength and flexibility.

Golf is not merely a strength game. Technique (neuromuscular coordination) and strategy are critical. As you develop additional levels of strength and endurance, you will see changes in both of these factors. For example, as you start hitting the ball farther and with more confidence, you can begin taking more straight-line approaches to the green rather than playing it safe and avoiding potential trouble spots. Thus, as you do the workouts, be attentive to your game and especially to your swing technique so that you can find a smooth blending of both.

Maintaining Your Gains

To ensure that there are no losses in your physical abilities, you should work out one or two days per week. Do one set of each exercise needed to enhance your swing, certain key actions, or just to keep your back strong. For troublesome areas, do two sets. The repetitions will vary depending on your level of fitness and goals. However, for most golfers, doing one set of the key exercises for ten to twenty RM is usually sufficient when done once or twice a week.

If you stop working out (or if you do not exercise to maintain your fitness levels), you may find your swing changing. This is especially true as you age. But by maintaining your strength and flexibility levels, you will be able to maintain the ability to swing basically the same way in the later years as in your youth. Increase your physical abilities, and you will play on a higher skill level.

For example, one of the biggest differences that I have seen with seniors, including tour players, is that they have not been able to maintain the same swing as when they were younger. Many of them lose strength and flexibility, especially in the hips and shoulders. They can still score well, mainly because of the constant practice and playing, which allows them to be more accurate in the short game and putting. But these golfers could play on even higher levels if they would undertake some of the specialized exercises presented in this book to regain and even improve their abilities.

Principles of Training

Working out can mean many things to different people, but how you work out is critical to your development. To get maximum results, you should adhere to the proven principles of exercise.

Individualization

You are a unique individual. Not only are you different in facial appearance, but also in your body composition and golf swing. Your body type is suitable for a particular swing and particular exercises that can improve your swing. Aside from the obvi-ous structural differences, there are also physiological differences in the muscular, circulatory, and nervous systems that require differences in your program. This is why you must be the one to make the final decision as to exactly which and how many exercises are needed and how many sets and reps should be done. Your training program should be for you and only you.

Even though you cannot change your genetic makeup, you can modify your strength, flexibility, and other qualities. I have worked with many golfers who have literally transformed their bodies and golf games. Some started off being fairly lackadaisical, but ended up being the most active exercisers (and golfers) I have ever seen. They developed enhanced movement skills that enabled them to play on a level where they got maximum enjoyment from the game.

Gradualness

Regardless of your exercise program or level of play, any increases in flexibility, strength, endurance, resistance, repetitions, or sets should be very gradual. For example, if you are accustomed to doing fifteen RM for two sets, you should not in one day change to fifty or sixty repetitions or do four sets. Your body is not ready for such abrupt changes, and because of this injuries may occur. This is one of the main reasons for injuries occurring to golfers—doing more than what your body is accustomed to. To prevent injury and to maximize your results, all gains should be gradual.

Progressiveness

In order to continually increase in muscular strength, endurance, or flexibility, you must progressively but gradually increase the amount of resistance (intensity), the number of exercises, or the total number of repetitions (volume) used. If you continue working at the same level and do the same number of exercises, sets, and reps, you will only maintain your achieved fitness level.

Overload

Overload means that you do more than what your body is accustomed to. In order to develop greater strength, you must use additional resistance. To increase flexibility, you must increase the range of motion. In the beginning stages of training, regardless of whether you increase resistance or repetitions, development will be approximately the same. Later these two qualities are very specific and must be trained separately.

There are also other ways to achieve overload. This includes increasing the rate of work, that is, doing the exercises at a slightly faster rate of speed or in an explosive manner. These methods, however, are only for more advanced golfers.

Awareness

To be aware of the changes taking place, you should keep a diary of your workouts. Record not only the resistance, sets, and repetitions for each exercise, but also how you feel. Make notations of what you experience, both mentally and physically.

This is especially important for women who respond differently in each of the phases of the menstrual cycle. Some women do their best work (or playing) before or after menstruation, while others perform better at the actual time of menstruation. Because of this, women should determine when they can do their most productive work and schedule the workouts (and playing) around the menstrual cycle. In general, stay away from very strenuous activity (such as using heavy resistance) during the menstrual period.

Awareness also means being cognizant of what is happening to your body. You should learn what each exercise feels like and how your body responds to it. In time, you will develop a muscle memory so that when you execute the exercise (or swing), you can tell immediately if it is working for you or if something is amiss. When things do not feel right, you should check to see if your execution is correct or if there is some other problem that is interfering.

Consistency

Without consistency in your exercise program, all the work that you do may come to naught. For example, after each workout, your energy supply is used up. It is replaced while you are resting and sleeping, and additional energy supplies for later use are deposited. This is known as supercompensation. If you do not exercise sufficiently to use this extra energy that has been deposited, the body will reabsorb it and as a result you may be left with the same energy as before. For example, I am sure you have noticed that when you have not played for awhile or have become sedentary, you actually become more tired than if you were active throughout the entire day.

Consistency, which means doing the exercises on a regular basis, is the key to success in any exercise program or golf game! This is the area in which I have found most golfers usually fail. What I recommend, therefore, is that you block off the time needed in your busy schedule so that the exercise program becomes as important as all your other activities.

Even though exercise is often given a low place in the scheme of priorities, it is the key to attaining and maintaining your health, fitness level, and golf swing. Being more fit allows you to get everything done more efficiently, enabling you to accomplish a greater number of activities. I am sure you have heard the expression, "If you want to get a job done, give it to a busy person."

Because consistency is so important, I formulated most of the exercises in this book using rubber tubing such as the Active Cords. The main reason for this is that you can carry the cords with you when you go away on vacation or on business. You can hook the rubber tubing up in a hotel room so that you can continue your workouts without interruption, and practice your swing movements as much as possible.

If for some reason you are unable to work out for a week or two, start your exercises again upon your return, using a little less resistance. In one or two days, you should get back into the groove of doing the exercises. So do not be overly concerned when situations arise that do not allow you to continue the program; however, do not allow this to happen on a regular basis.

If you want to improve your game in the shortest amount of time, schedule the exercises you should do. Once you set up a regular exercise program, you will see the benefits quite soon. It is at this time that you will become hooked. You will look forward to doing the exercises because you will see what the exercises are doing for you and how they are improving your swing and game. You will also experience greater confidence in yourself, which will transfer to your game and everyday life.

Services Available

If you would like personalized help to improve your swing or golf game, Sports Training, Inc. and I are happy to offer the following services:

- Biomechanical analysis of your swing
- Analysis of your physical abilities
- A personalized exercise program
- Technique enhancement
- Nutritional counseling
- Improving the mental side of your game
- Exercise equipment

Work can be done in person or via videotapes and audiotapes. Also, for information on any of the equipment used in this book or for a record-keeping book, please contact:

Sports Training, Inc.
P.O. Box 460429
Escondido, CA 92046
Telephone: (760) 480-0558 or (877) Dr Yessis
Fax: (760) 480-1277
E-Mail: sptstrng@aol.com
website: http://www.dryessis.com

CHAPTER

14

The Exercise Program
Basic Maintenance

Helpful Tips to Maintain Your Exercise Program

Most golfers are successful in initiating an exercise program, but tend to keep it up for only relatively short periods of time. Because of this, they rarely see the positive results that are possible. To prevent this from happening to you and to help you maintain your program, following are some time-proven tips that have worked successfully for many golfers:

Schedule Exercise (and Golf) First

When you decide to exercise and to play golf, these activities should receive top priority. This may seem heretical, as it appears to take away from your work, family, and other aspects of your life that are extremely important. However, setting time aside to exercise is a key element in guaranteeing your success. It will also positively influence other areas of your life.

For example, by maintaining your exercise program, your mental work will improve. This in turn makes you more efficient and productive, which then allows you to get more done. This saves you

time, makes you feel better, and allows you to play more and better golf. Putting exercise and golf in only when you have time will doom you to defeat.

The Exercise Lifestyle

Exercise and golf should be a part of your healthy lifestyle. In essence, you must develop the habit of participation on a regular basis. Once the habit is established, it is very difficult to break. But in order to establish the habit, it must become a part of your normal, everyday routine.

Give Exercise (and Golf) a Fair Chance

First exposure to any new sport or exercise program can be uncomfortable. This also holds true for many other areas of life. However, continuing in the activity and having effective instruction in learning the basic skills can lead to enjoyment and pleasure. Keep in mind that very few activities are truly enjoyed from the very first day of participation. You learn to enjoy the activity! This takes time. For golf, it usually takes until you can hit the ball well most of the time.

Start Slowly

Your body needs time to adapt in order for the gains to be seen, and, most importantly, for the gains to last. Progress in the program can be fast, but any increases in volume, intensity, exercises, and so on should be slow and gradual.

Keep It Individualized

The training program must be individualized to fit you. This means that you should make progress at your own rate and that the training program must be based on your capabilities—not on someone else's.

Just Do It

People are great at making up excuses for why they cannot play or exercise. They procrastinate and say they will do it at a later time. This is acceptable at times, but chronic procrastination can defeat all good intentions.

Skipping one or two workouts can be quickly made up. But if you start skipping more days, it is important to figure out why and what remedial steps can be taken immediately. Not only does procrastinating jeopardize the success of any program, it is also stressful and lowers your self-esteem, further snuffing your motivation to stick with the program.

Keep a Workout Diary

When you keep a diary of the workouts, either by yourself or in conjunction with others, it can be used to evaluate your progress. The record keeping book should show whether progress is commensurate with your abilities and whether any problems are developing along the way. Constant reference to the diary with evaluation is very beneficial.

Get a Feel for the Exercise or the Skills Involved

You should be cognizant of what changes are taking place and learn to experience the feel of the exercise not only in the muscles, but also mentally. The key here is to recognize the changes and actions that produce the good feelings or results.

Forget About Being Perfect

Many golfers look for perfection. Even youngsters hesitate to undertake an activity if they do not feel they can do it perfectly. The key here is to participate and not always be concerned with the outcome. You should participate to get the enjoyment from the activity, not only to achieve a certain level of fitness or golf score.

Half a Workout Is Better Than None

If it is impossible to have a full workout, doing a partial one is still of great benefit. Flexibility here is as important mentally as it is physically.

Give It Six to Eight Weeks

Six to eight weeks is the amount of time it takes to develop a new habit. It is also how long it takes before you experience the physiological changes in the body as a result of the exercise program. These are the long-lasting benefits that usually hook you on the activity and incline you toward greater participation.

Variety Is the Spice of Life

The fastest way to get stale is to do the same thing day after day. If you are involved in the same exercises on a daily or every-other-day basis, you will probably get bored with the activity, and the body and mind will become stagnant. Thus, performing a variety of exercises (in relation to your swing) is extremely beneficial in continually motivating yourself and creating ways in which you can gain greater satisfaction.

Do Not Obsess over Food

Proper nutrition is critical to the best performances. However, being obsessive in relation to what and how much you eat is a detriment to producing a healthy lifestyle. Avoid thinking in terms of good foods or bad foods; instead, think variety. All foods have value. The main items to beware of are the saturated fats, trans-fatty acids, and processed foods.

Set Realistic Goals

When goals are realistic, they can be attained. You can then achieve the success and satisfaction needed to drive you on.

Give It Your Best Try

Exercise and golf participation require hard work, not only in the learning process but also in improving your ability. When you realize that it takes hard work to achieve the gains that you desire, you will be more inclined to do the work to get the many benefits. Tell yourself it will be worth it; remind yourself of the benefits.

Just Get Started

The most difficult part of an exercise or sports program is taking the first step. Once it is taken, however, you overcome much of your anxiety and can then get into the activity. By making this start, you will feel like continuing.

Do What Is Enjoyable

If you do not enjoy the activities in which you participate, you will quit. For example, golf may not include all components of health-related fitness, but it is still superior to starting and then quitting other "fitness" activities that may include all the components. The key is to be active and to do exercises that can help you, regardless of whether they achieve all of your goals at one time.

Say, "Yes, I Can"

Research shows that affirmations, simple positive statements that reflect your beliefs and intents, are powerful ways to keep on track or to change for the better. When you think positively, you will get positive results. The goal is to focus on the process of making positive changes and on improvements, not on perfection. Replace negative thoughts with positive ones. If you do not believe you can succeed, your program will be doomed to failure. The great thing about exercise and golf is that they are not just ends in themselves. They are a means of helping to achieve other things in life through a balanced, healthy lifestyle.

Keep an Eye on the Future

Focus more closely on where your swing or fitness level will be in the next few months, or even years. If you keep your goals in mind, especially long-term goals, you will be more likely to succeed and not be set back by minor failures. This is a great way to maintain a positive, long-range outlook.

Visualize Success

When you see yourself performing well in your imagination, it helps to increase your self-confidence. If you can see it and believe it, it can be realized.

A Final Word

In conclusion, as you get involved in your golf improvement program, keep in mind that everyone can improve. It is extremely rare (if even possible) to find a golfer with the perfect swing. But there is an ideal swing that you can strive for. To succeed, you need to capture the key elements of the swing. They will far overpower your weaker points and thus enable you to achieve high levels of success. Remember, even the best professional golfers have room for improvement. Just as they can play some great rounds of golf, so can you. I sincerely hope this book will be your guide to a successful swing—a swing that is as good as your physical abilities allow. As a result, you will get the most enjoyment and satisfaction from your game.

Index